Monograph Series of the Socio-Economic History Society, Japan

This monograph series is published by the Socio-Economic History Society, Japan, and Springer.

The aim of the series is to make works by Japanese scholars accessible to a wider readership and thereby enhance the global knowledge of Japanese and Asian scholarship in the fields of economic, social, and business history.

This book series will present English translations of outstanding recent academic research works, survey articles, and book reviews carefully selected from the Society's quarterly Japanese-language journal *Socio-Economic History*, which is the preeminent journal in its field in Japan, as well as from other publications of the Society. These will be edited under specific themes such as energy and the environment, the consumer society and the company system in postwar Japan, and the economic history of Japan in the early twentieth century. The content will include chapters on economic, social, and business history ranging geographically from Japan and Asia as a whole to Europe and the United States, and a small number of book reviews of recent academic works published in Japanese and other languages.

The Society was founded in 1930 and currently comprises more than 1400 registered members, mainly academics, researchers and postgraduate students affiliated with universities and research institutions in Japan.

More information about this series at http://www.springer.com/series/13569

Satoshi Baba
Editor

Economic History of Cities and Housing

Springer

Editor
Satoshi Baba
Graduate School of Economics
The University of Tokyo
Bunkyo-ku, Tokyo, Japan

ISSN 2364-2394 ISSN 2364-2408 (electronic)
Monograph Series of the Socio-Economic History Society, Japan
ISBN 978-981-10-4096-2 ISBN 978-981-10-4097-9 (eBook)
DOI 10.1007/978-981-10-4097-9

Library of Congress Control Number: 2017938581

Printed on acid-free paper

This Springer imprint is published by Springer Nature
The registered company is Springer Nature Singapore Pte Ltd.
The registered company address is: 152 Beach Road, #21-01/04 Gateway East, Singapore 189721, Singapore

Preface

This book is the fourth volume in a monograph series published by the Socio-Economic History Society, Japan, and Springer. It contains four recent articles and four short book reviews of recent academic Japanese-language works, all on topics related to the history of cities and housing.

Urban history is an important area of socio-economic history that interacts with a wide range of other disciplines, including jurisprudence, public administration, economics, sociology, geography and architectonics. Previously, most historians in Europe and Japan focused on the medieval period, but recently, there has been increasing interest in the period from the eighteenth century onwards because of the deep impact that industrialization had on urbanization. There has been particular interest in the cities of the twentieth century because of the many changes that occurred in both urban policy and systems of municipal administration during this period. The high population density of the twentieth-century city produced a wide range of problems including unemployment and sanitation that could not be solved by local governments alone. The provision of adequate housing was an area where central government had a particularly important role to play. However, ordinary citizens also participated in finding solutions to these problems, as members of voluntary associations or city councilors.

The first two articles discuss urban formation and housing in Japan during the mid-twentieth century. Chapter 1, by Numajiri, uses the case of Amagasaki City in Hyogo Prefecture to examine the implementation of land readjustment in the period from the beginning of the Second Sino-Japanese War in 1937 up to the period of reform that followed World War II. Although tenant cultivation rights were strengthened during the war years, laws and regulations concerning city planning were not revised to take this into account. As a result, conflicts occurred between landowners and tenant farmers when land readjustment projects were resumed. The former were successful in litigation against the latter, allowing the reallocation of agricultural land for public use. Nevertheless, tenant farmers were able to retain land for agricultural use within newly formed urban areas. This is an important characteristic of urban formation in Japan.

Chapter 2, by Ono, examines the reconstruction of the living spaces devastated during World War II through a case study of Tokyo in the late 1940s. The author also provides a historical account of the reconstruction process from the perspective of the creation and distribution of private residential space under the postwar Japanese regulatory regime. Residential rent controls protected tenants of rented accommodation that had escaped wartime destruction but dealt a fatal blow to the housing supply system that was in place at the time. Moreover, rent controls and heavy taxation meant that many rented units turned into owner-occupied houses. Consequently, an enormous number of people found that they could not live in Tokyo unless they could find rooms to rent through personal connections. Since living spaces became increasingly crowded and the existing housing stock was not properly maintained, there was a sharp deterioration of housing standards in Japan.

The next two articles are concerned with urban social policy and urban industry in twentieth-century Europe. Chapter 3, by Mori, examines the adoption of communal unemployment insurance systems in Wilhelminian Germany through case studies of two cities in the Greater Berlin Administration Union. The most well-known system of communal unemployment insurance was the Genter system, under which the city paid subsidies to trade unions so that they could provide their out-of-work members with unemployment benefits. But the introduction of the system varied according to the circumstances of individual cities, and Schöneberg was the only city adjoining Berlin to establish such a system, in 1911. A similar system was proposed in Charlottenburg, but was rejected by the city council. Communal unemployment insurance systems in Germany were local attempts to tackle the problem of unemployment before the enactment of the German Unemployment Insurance Act of 1927. They are typical examples of the way in which cities played a pioneering role in the emergence of the welfare state.

Chapter 4, by Nakajima, examines the development of the mechanical engineering industry in the Paris region in the period from 1939 to 1958. Mechanical engineering in this area was reactivated by the policy of rearmament introduced from 1935. Despite stagnation during the Vichy period and the unsettled situation immediately after the war, it blossomed in the early 1950s. The manufacture of aircraft engines, industrial motors and machine tools were the leading sectors. The concentration of the French mechanical engineering industry in the Paris region is worthy of attention because of the thick *tissu industriel* from assemblers to suppliers and from finishers to intermediate processors all collected in the same region. It can be seen as a typical case of the development of urban industry through industry clusters.

The four book reviews also deal with recent Japanese-language studies in the fields of urban and housing history. They are an empirical investigation into land development in a suburban area of Tokyo in the mid-twentieth century by Shūichi Takashima (Chap. 5); the results of a collaborative research project on British urban history in the 'long' eighteenth century (Chap. 6) edited by Tadashi Nakano, Tatsuyuki Karasawa and Ichirō Michishige; a pioneering work on Czech housing policy and social history in the first half of the twentieth century by Yoshiyuki Morishita (Chap. 7); and a detailed study of German housing problems and non-profit housing in the 1920s that focuses on the case of the city of Solingen by Nodoka Nagayama (Chap. 8).

I would like to thank Professor Helen Ballhatchet, who translated Chaps. 1 and 5 and checked the Preface and Chaps. 3 and 4; Dr. Kōichi Inaba, who translated Chap. 2; Ms. Louisa Rubinfien, who checked Chaps. 2 and 7; and Ms. Ruth Fallon, who checked Chaps. 6 and 8.

Tokyo, Japan Satoshi Baba

Contents

Contributors

Satoshi Baba is a professor at the University of Tokyo. He obtained a Ph.D. in economics from the University of Tokyo. His main research field is the economic and urban history of modern Europe. His publications include *Doitsu Nōson Kōgyōshi* (Proto-Industrialization in Germany) (University of Tokyo Press, 1993) and *Doitsu Toshikeikaku no Shakaikeizaishi* (Social and Economic History of Town Planning in Germany) (University of Tokyo Press, 2016).

Takahito Mori is an associate professor at Hitotsubashi University. He obtained a Ph.D. in social sciences from Hitotsubashi University in 2005. His main research field is the socio-economic history of modern Germany. His publications include *Elektrifizierung als Urbanisierungsprozess: Frankfurt am Main 1886–1933* (Darmstadt, 2014) and *Doitsu Kindai Toshi Shakai Keizaishi* (Socio-economic History of German City) (Nihon Keizai Hyôronsha, 2009).

Nodoka Nagayama is an associate professor at Aoyama Gakuin University. She obtained a Ph.D. in economics from Hitotsubashi University in 2008. Her main research field is the economic history of Germany. Her publications include *Doitsu Jyūtaku Mondai no Shakai Keizai shi teki Kenkyū* (Study on the Socio-economic History of Housing Problems in Germany) (Nihon Keizai Hyōronsha, 2012).

Toshikatsu Nakajima is a professor at Rikkyo University. He obtained a Ph.D. in history from Paris-Sorbonne University in 1985. His main research field is the modern economic history of France. His publications include *French Economic Plans and the Mechanical Engineering Industry in the Paris Region, 1953–1974*, in Patrick Fridenson and Dominique Barjot (eds.), *France-Japon, regards croisés* (Presses de l'Université Paris-Sorbonne, 2015), and *Le transfert de la technologie des machines-outils français au Japon (1952–1962)*, in Serge Benoît and Alain P. Michel (eds.), *Le monde du génie industriel au XXe siècle: Autour de Pierre Bézier et des machines-outils* (Pôle éditorial de l'Université de technologie de Belfort-Montbéliard, 2015).

Akinobu Numajiri is a professor at Rikkyo University. He obtained a Ph.D. in economics from the University of Tokyo in 1999. His main research field is the socio-economic history of modern Japan. His publications include *Sonraku kara mita Shigaichi Keisei: Hito to Tochi · Mizu no Kankeishi Amagasaki, 1925–1973* (The Process of Urban Formation as Seen from Rural Communities: The History of Relationships Between the People and the Land and Water in Amagasaki, 1925–1973) (Nihon Keizai Hyōronsha, 2015).

Hiroshi Ono is an associate professor of economics at Kumamoto Gakuen University. He obtained a Ph.D. in economics from Rikkyo University in 2007. His main research field is the economic history of Japan. His publications include *Jūkūkan no Keizaishi* (The Economic History of Living Spaces) (Nihon Keizai Hyōronsha, 2014).

Minoru Yasumoto is a professor emeritus at Komazawa University. He obtained a Ph.D. in economics from Keio University. His main research field is the economic and social history and historical demography of modern Britain. His publications include *Industrialisation, Urbanisation and Demographic Change in England* (The University of Nagoya Press, 1994) and *The Rise of a Victorian Ironopolis: Middlesbrough and Regional Industrialization* (Boydell & Brewer, 2011).

Part I
Economic and Social History of Cities and Housing in Japan and Europe

Chapter 1
Landowners and Tenant Farmers in the Process of Urban Formation: A Case Study of Amagasaki City, Hyogo Prefecture, 1937–1952

Akinobu Numajiri

Abstract This study aims to clarify the characteristics of the urbanization that occurred under the land readjustment projects implemented in the period from the Sino-Japanese War to the reforms following World War II, by focusing on the conflict between landowners and tenant farmers in Amagasaki city, Hyogo prefecture. The following are the three points examined:

The first point explains how arable land within land readjustment sites was actually used during the war. Landowners paid the tenant farmers compensation money before land readjustment projects were implemented. In this case study, however, projects fell behind due to the lack of materials, thus allowing the peasants to continue farming.

The second point involves the conflict between landowners and tenant farmers during the period of the post-war reforms. The conflict was over replotting and reduction of arable land, both of which the tenant farmers opposed. In the end, the claims made by the landowners who followed government policy were accepted.

The third point presents the characteristics of urbanized areas. The implementation of land readjustment projects caused the reduction of arable land, creating instead land for public use. Nevertheless, the tenant farmers influenced the formation of urban areas by continuing to use land for farming with the approval of the Agricultural Committee, the local authority that oversees agricultural issues.

Keywords Farming household • Land readjustment • Land reform • Landowners • Tenant farmer • Urban formation

---

This chapter is a translation of an article that originally appeared in *Shakai Keizai Shigaku* 77(1) (May 2011), pp. 3–23.

A. Numajiri (✉)
College of Arts, Rikkyo University,
3-34-1, Nishi-ikebukuro, Toshima-ku, 171-8501 Tokyo, Japan
e-mail: numajiri@rikkyo.ac.jp

S. Baba (ed.), *Economic History of Cities and Housing*, Monograph Series of the Socio-Economic History Society, Japan, DOI 10.1007/978-981-10-4097-9_1

1 Introduction

This chapter uses a case study of Amagasaki city in Hyogo prefecture to examine the process of land readjustment under Article 12 of the 1919 City Planning Act from 1937, the beginning of the Sino-Japanese War, until the end of the post-war reform period in 1952. The purpose is to clarify the characteristics of urban formation as seen from agricultural villages. The author's reason for focusing on agricultural villages is to examine land readjustment projects that targeted areas on the outskirts of cities where urban formation was slow. These were carried out on a wide scale by non-government associations. The chapter will show how the various interests and demands of landowners, who were responsible for the projects, and tenant farmers, who were the users of the land at the time when the projects began, affected first, the actual progress of the projects, and second, the nature of the urban land that was formed as a result.

Historical research into city planning in modern Japan has examined the legal system and the various concepts of city planning itself. Ishida Yorifusa (2004) and Harada Sumitaka (2001) drew attention to the fact that the process was led by the state, while Koshizawa Akira (1991), for example, looked at the actual planning proposals and those who produced them. On the other hand, Iwami Ryōtarō (1978) pointed out that on the outskirts of large cities it was landowners who promoted land readjustment, and revealed the various problems that occurred because of the links between urban planning and their interests as a class. The author of this chapter has also written about the role of landowners in regulating the supply-demand relationship for factory land, and the effect that this had on urban planning (Numajiri 2002). Recently there has been an increase in empirical case studies of this kind, leading to further examination of the role of landowners as non-government agents in urban planning. The field of enquiry has also widened, for example, into consideration of changes in the functioning of local communities (Suzuki 2004; Takashima 2003, 2004). The author himself has used a case study of the associations in the Amagasaki area in the 1930s to demonstrate both the leading role of resident landowners in producing public land as part of land readjustment, and the development of privately held residential land in readjustment areas, including the various problems that arose as a result (Numajiri 2008).

However, all these recent studies on landowners as agents in land readjustment, including those of the author himself, have tended to focus on the 1920s and 1930s. This is despite the fact that there was significant growth in the number of land readjustment associations in the second half of the 1930s, in relation to the wartime need to develop manufacturing capacity (Numajiri 2002, pp. 137–138). In some cases, the projects being carried out by these associations were not completed before the end of the war.

Of importance here is the fact that the period 1937–1952 saw a strengthening in the cultivation rights of the tenant farmers, the existing users of the land, so that where land readjustment projects were unfinished, various conflicts occurred between them and landowners (Nōsei Chōsakai 1956), causing new problems in

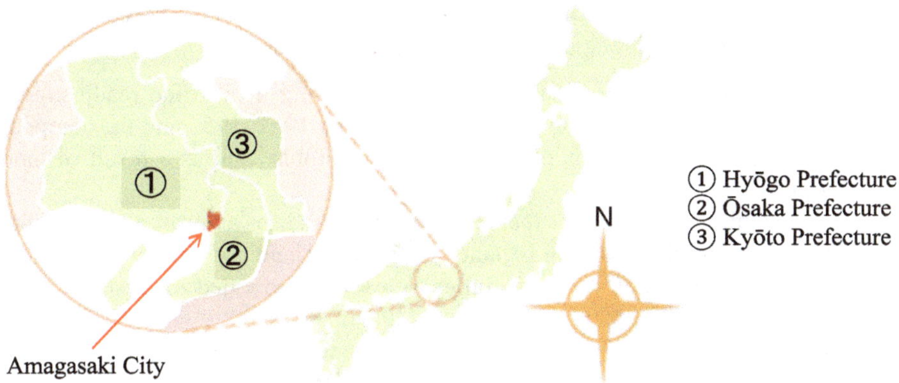

Fig. 1.1 The geography of Amagasaki City (*Source*: Amagasaki Municipal Office, The official website of Amagasaki. Retrieved on January 2016 from http://www.city.amagasaki.hyogo.jp/sogo_annai/003_chisei.html)

urban planning. In other words, as a result of this legal strengthening of cultivation rights, land readjustment became subject to conflicts between a), the tenant farmers, who stressed their rights under the Agricultural Land Reform Acts that gave owner farmers a public role, and b), the landowners, who justified land readjustment as a method of urban planning. Through paying attention to these conflicts, it should be possible to clarify the logic behind urban formation in land readjustment areas and therefore demonstrate how the strengthening of peasants' cultivation rights changed the nature of urban formation in agricultural villages on city outskirts. This chapter will therefore shed light on an aspect of urban formation that is very different from the focus of those like Ishida, whose interest has been mainly on plans for post-war urban regeneration and who has therefore concentrated on the role of the state.[1]

Therefore, this chapter will examine the land readjustment associations established by landowners in the war period and focus on the conflicts of interest between landowners and tenant farmers, particularly regarding the use of agricultural land and compensation payments. This should help to reveal the significance of land readjustment projects and agricultural land use during urban formation. It examines the Ōshō-chūbudaiichi[2] Land Readjustment Association of Ōshō village in the district of Muko, which was adjacent to Amagasaki city (Fig. 1.1), a city representative of those that had rapidly urbanized as a result of the growth of industrialisation in the 1920s and 1930s (Ōishi and Kanazawa 2003), with a special focus on one particular area in the village, Hamada. The association was among those that were formed in rapid succession on the outskirts of the city during the Sino-Japanese war,

[1] For a previous work that sheds light on such villages, see Ebato (1987).

[2] This association was originally called Ōshōmura-chūbudaiichi, but *mura* (village) was removed from its name after the incorporation of the village into Amagasaki in 1942. In this chapter, Ōshō-chūbudaiichi will be used throughout.

Ōshō village itself being incorporated into Amagasaki in 1942. The chapter will focus on the following three points regarding the association:

(a) Through analysing the actual conditions of farming in wartime readjustment areas, it will clarify the state of cultivation during 1937–1952 and the compensation paid to tenant farmers who would lose arable land as a result of land readjustment.
(b) It will examine the problems that occurred in Hamada as an example of conflict between the implementation of land readjustment and the demands of tenant farmers for cultivation rights, in order to reveal the divided interests of landowners and tenant farmers and the final outcome.
(c) Finally, it will consider how the demands of the tenant farmers left their special mark on the urban formation of the first half of the 1950s, despite their exclusion from membership of readjustment associations.[3]

2 Arable Land and the Expansion of Land Readjustment in the War Period

2.1 Land Readjustment in the Area Around Tachibana Station

Designation of areas for urban planning in Amagasaki and its surroundings was carried out in 1925, but the work of land readjustment associations did not really take off until the 1930s. Figure 1.2 shows the land readjustment area for Tachibana station and its surroundings. Land readjustment progressed smoothly along with the building of the new station. For example, the Tachibana Land Readjustment Association (Fig. 1.2a) that was established in 1933 had finished construction work in the area by 1937 and in 1940 the number of buildings reached 1700 (KKa). The success of this project was accompanied by an increase in both the population and in house building, and land readjustment associations were established in quick succession in the surrounding areas. Among them were the Tachibana-daini Association (Fig. 1.2b), set up in May 1938 and covering 39.9 ha, the Ōshō-chūbudaiichi Association (Fig. 1.2c), set up in October 1939 and covering 118.7 ha, and the Tachibana-ikushima Association (Fig. 1.2d, set up in December 1939 and covering 63.8 ha (Amagasakishi Toshikyoku Keikakubu Toshikeikakuka 1992).

The initiative in founding each of these associations came from landowners, who were motivated by the rise in land values that took place in readjustment areas. The

[3] Land readjustment projects carried out by non-governmental associations were based on Article 12 of the 1919 City Planning Act, and implemented in accordance with the provisions of the Arable Land Consolidation Act. For official recognition, associations for land readjustment required the agreement of over half the total number of landowners in the area providing that they represented over two thirds of the total area and total value of the land therein. However, tenant farmers who cultivated the land but did not own any could not become members (Okazaki 1925).

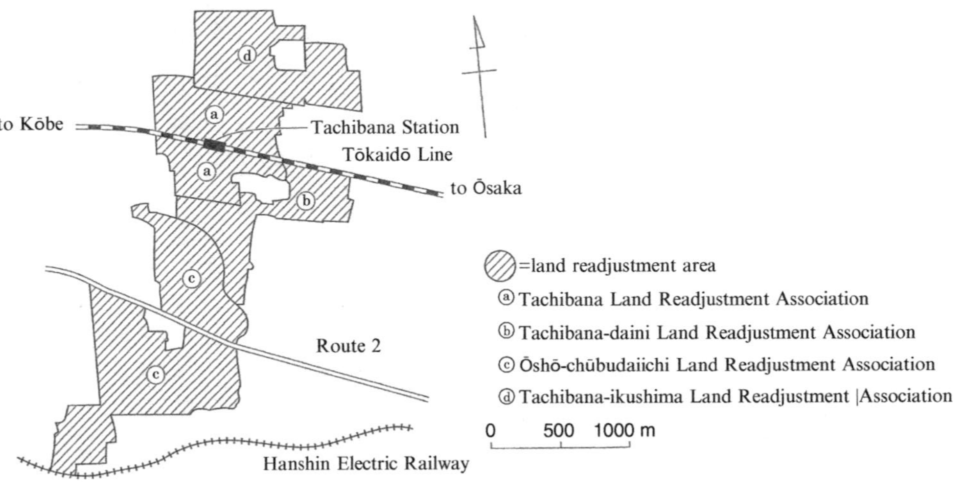

Fig. 1.2 Location of land readjustment association set up around Tachibana Station in the 1930s (*Source*: Amagasaki Toshikyoku Keikakubu Toshikeikakuka (1992), p. 101)

Tachibana Association had 214 parcels of reserve land[4] comprising 7.2 ha with a selling price of from 3 to 18 yen/m^2, with prices in the 6–9 yen range being the most common. In view of the fact that the value of land in the same area before land readjustment was around 0.6–1.5 yen/m^2, it is clear that the land was now being valued as residential land for sale purposes. It should also be noted that almost all of the reserve land had been sold by 1936 (Numajiri 2008). Associations in the surrounding areas also expected to profit through the revaluation of arable land as residential land. The total estimated income of the Tachibana-daini Association was 861,426 yen, of which 515,600 yen, 59.9% of the total estimate, was the selling price of reserve land (KKb); in the case of the Ōshō-chūbudaiichi Association, the total estimated income was 1,901,935 yen, with 1,044,380 yen, 73.8% of the total estimate, being the selling price of reserve land (KKc). In other words, associations planned to raise over half of the income for the readjustment projects from sales of reserve land. The rise in the average price of land per square metre from the 7.6 yen estimated for Tachibana-daini in 1938 (KKb) to the 12.1 yen estimated for Ōshō-chūbudaiichi in 1940 (KKc) shows how the urbanization of the surroundings of Tachibana Station encouraged development plans in neighbouring areas, in expectation of rising land prices.

2.2 *Landowners and Peasants in the Ōshō-chūbudaiichi Land Readjustment Area*

During the 1930s, the population of the village of Ōshō rose rapidly, from 9536 in 1930, to 16,071 in 1935 and to 39,149 in 1940 (Enomoto 1942). The main cause was the development of manufacturing in the city of Amagasaki and in the village itself. In view of this increase, the Ōshō-chūbudaiichi Land Readjustment Association designated almost the whole of the area of Hamada, and parts of Higashi-ōshima, Higashi, and Nishi for land readjustment (KKc). As is clear from Fig. 1.2, the Ōshō-chūbudaiichi land readjustment area was situated to the south of the Tachibana area, with the Hanshin (Ōsaka-Kōbe) highway crossing through the middle. Before land readjustment began there were 241 landowners. The main ones are listed in Table 1.1. Along with absentee landowners, including companies such as Matsuoka Kisen (Matsuoka Shipping) and Hanshin Denki Tetsudō (Hanshin Electric Railway) and Kashimoto Buhei, a resident of Amagasaki, there were also residents who were landowners. In particular, it is clear that there were a large number of residential landowners in Hamada, for example, Horimoto Genjirō and Hori Shigeru. Even if we disregard the landholdings of Hanshin Denki Tetsudō, which are unknown, owners of 2 ha of land or more accounted for 47% of the total area. In 1942, the land categories of the total amount of privately owned land in the

[4]"Reserve land" refers to areas that were removed in advance from the plans for replotting when readjustment projects were implemented. These areas of land were made available for sale by the individual readjustment associations, as a source of funding for the projects.

Table 1.1 Land Ownership of Ōshō-chūbudaiichi Land Readjustment Association members owning more than 2 ha (before readjustment began) (Units: ha, %)

Owner's name	Area owned	Percentage of the total area	Additional comments
Ōshō Village, Muko District	8.9	7.9	
Matsuoka Kisen (Matsuoka Shipping)	6.8	6.0	
Horimoto Genjirō	5.9	5.3	Resident of Hamada
Kashimoto Buhei	5.6	5.0	Large taxpayer; resident of Nishiyama-cho, Amagasaki city
Hori Shigeru	4.8	4.2	Resident of Hamada
Ba Heisan	3.2	2.8	Resident of Fukiai-ku, Kobe city
Yanagawa Shōitsu	3.0	2.7	Resident of Higashishinden
Horiuchi Kametarō	2.9	2.6	Resident of Hamada
Miyazaki Ichirōbei	2.9	2.6	Resident of Higashishinden
Kusaba Chūbei	2.5	2.2	Resident of Hamada
Konishi Sukeuemon	2.4	2.2	
Terada Zentarō	2.4	2.1	Resident of Higashishinden
Tanaka Kichitarō	2.2	1.9	Resident of Hamada
Hanshin Denki Tetsudō (Hanshin Electric Railway)	–	–	

Sources: Ōshō-chūbudaiichi Tochi Kukaku Seiri Kumiai

Note: Due to damage to the source material, some parts could not be deciphered. The unreadable parts included details of the area owned by Hanshin Denki Tetsudō (Hanshin Electric Railway), but it was possible to decipher that the rent value of the land was over 1000 yen, which means that the area must have been over 2 ha. The name of the company has therefore been included here

Ōshō-chūbudaiichi land readjustment area (126.7 ha) were "rice fields" (92.2 ha), "fields for other crops" (2.0 ha) and "residential land" (21.7 ha). In other words, in terms of land categories, the main use was as arable land.

The features of the farming households in Hamada can be shown through examination of a survey of 1938. The total number of farming households in Ōshō village was 398, of which 41 were in Hamada. The total number of households registered in Hamada for the same year was 176, with 1219 temporary residents (Enomoto 1942), indicating that the majority of households were already not engaged in farming. The breakdown of owner and tenant farmers in the village as a whole was 68 owner farmers, 85 that owned some land but were also tenants, and 245 full tenants, showing a high ratio of tenants, but the corresponding figures for Hamada, of 9, 2 and 30 respectively, show a particularly high ratio of tenants. In addition, in Hamada itself only two farming households were cultivating land of 1 ha or more, with about half being small-scale tenant farmers cultivating arable land of less than 0.5 ha (ŌYa).

Table 1.2 shows a breakdown of the 41 farming households in Hamada according to indices such as the extent of their dependence on income from farming, the area of land cultivated and the level of tenancy, the number of buildings owned, class as

Table 1.2 Characteristics of farming households in Hamada (Units: ha, %, no. of buildings)

Identifying number	Farming as a source of income (1938): either sole, main or partial	Sources of income other than farming (1938)	Area of land under cultivation (1938)	Ratio of tenant farming (%)	No. of buildings (houses, 1938)	No. of buildings (sheds, 1933)	No. of buildings (other/unclear, 1933)	Class according to *kyōgihi* contributions[a]	Member of Ōshō-chūbudaiichi Land Readjustment Association[b]
#1	Main	Hired labour	0.7	100	—	—	—	k	
#2	Main	Hired labour	0.4	100	1	1	0	l	
#3	Main	Hired labour	0.5	100	1	0	0	l	
#4	Sole		0.6	100	—	—	—	—	
#5	Sole		0.5	100	1	1	—	l	○
#6	Main	Hired labour	0.7	100	1	1	0	g	○
#7	Main	Hired labour	0.7	100	1	1	0	j	
#8	Sole		0.6	100	1	—	—	l	
#9	Sole		0.4	100	1	1	0	k	
#10	Sole		0.5	100	1	1	0	k	○
#11	Main	Other	0.3	100	—	—	—	—	
#12	Main	Commerce	0.6	100	1	1	0	g	○
#13	Sole		0.5	100	1	0	0	l	
#14	Partial	Other	0.2	100	2	1	1	d	○
#15	Main	Commerce	0.4	100	3	1	0	—	
#16	Partial	Commerce	0.1	100	1	0	0	l	
#17	Sole		0.6	100	1	1	0	i	
#18	Sole		0.9	100	—	—	—	—	
#19	Sole		0.4	0	2	1	0	—	○
#20	Sole		1.0	0	1	1	0	b	○
#21	Sole		1.1	0	1	1	2	a	○ 2 ha or more

#22	Partial	Other	0.1	0	3	1	2	—	○2 ha or more
#23	Main	Hired labour	0.6	0	3	1	3	a	○
#24	Main	Commerce	0.5	100	2	1	0	l	
#25	Partial	Other	0.5	0	7	2	4	a	○ 2 ha or more
#26	Main	Other	0.2	100	1	1	0	h	○
#27	Main	Other	0.5	55	1	1	1	b	○
#28	Partial	Commerce	0.2	100	—	—	—	—	
#29	Main	Hired labour	0.6	100	—	—	—	l	
#30	Sole		0.6	0	3	1	4	a	○ 2 ha or more
#31	Sole		0.4	100	—	—	—	—	
#32	Sole		0.3	100	—	—	—	—	
#33	Main	Hired labour	0.3	100	—	—	—	—	
#34	Main	Hired labour	0.3	0	1	1	2	e	○
#35	Partial	Other	0.3	0	1	1	6	a	○ 2 ha or more
#36	Main	Commerce	0.2	100	3	0	0	h	
#37	Sole		0.6	100	—	—	—	—	
#38	Partial	Industrial	0.2	100	—	—	—	k	
#39	Main	Commerce	0.4	80	2	1	1	e	○
#40	Partial	Other	0.1	100	0	1	0	l	
#41	Main	Hired labour	0.1	100	—	—	—	—	

Sources: ŌYa (1938); ŌYb (1934); Ōshōmura Hamada (1939); Ōshō-chūbudaiichi Tochi Kukaku Seiri Kumiai

Notes: "Area of land under cultivation" is the total area cultivated by each household including land outside Hamada

____ indicates that sources could not be found for the household in question

[a]The letters of the alphabet are explained in Table 1.3

[b]Members are indicated by ○: "2 ha or more" has been added to indicate members possessing land of 2 ha or more

indicated by contributions to *kyōgihi* (community expenses that were not counted as municipal expenditure), and membership of the Ōshō-chūbudaiichi Land Readjustment Association. Class is shown as letters of the alphabet, but details of the actual *kyōgihi* contribution for each class are given in Table 1.3. *Kyōgihi* in Hamada consisted of a land-tax rate plus a buildings rate. Since there was no direct link to income, in this chapter the levels of *kyōgihi* contributions given in Table 1.3 are used only to indicate class in terms of land ownership.

Analysis of this information shows the existence of three clear characteristics:

First, while the overall area of arable land per household in Hamada is small, when the range of *kyōgihi* contributions from "a" to "l" that is given in Table 1.3 is applied to the households in Table 1.2, it is clear that households #21, #23, #25, #30, and #35 are "upper" class. In terms of the amount of arable land per household, #21 has 1.1 ha, but the others are owner famers with less than 1 ha. However, it is clear from Table 1.1 that four out of these five households are landowners of more than 2 ha in the overall Ōshō-chūbudaiichi readjustment area. As in the case of #25, it should be noted that they have several buildings. This is probably because in addition to buildings inhabited by the household, they also have buildings to rent. The fact that the additional, non-farming, income of #25 and #30 is listed as "other" rather than as hired labour or commerce and industry also suggests that this income comes from renting buildings.

Second, in the case of tenant farmers, the tenanted land is 100% arable land. In most cases, the ownership of buildings was limited to one or two for the use of the household, or no buildings were owned at all. In addition, most of these households were at the lower end of the range of classes as indicated by *kyōgihi* contributions, being listed as j, k, or l, and, as Table 1.3 shows, few of these "lower-class" households were paying any land tax. Since the prewar regulations for arable land readjustment limited membership of land readjustment associations to those who owned land in the adjustment area, some farmers who were tenants in Hamada itself, including #5, #6, #10, and #12, were members, but there are as many as 23 tenant households, such as #1, #2, #3, and #4, whose membership cannot be ascertained. These include households such as #1, #4, #11, and #18 that did not own any land or buildings. Among those tenant farmers that were members, apart from household #12, none had more than 0.05 ha. Their land ownership was probably limited to land needed for buildings used by the household. In other words, there was a wide gap between such tenant farmers and landowners of 2 ha or more.

Third, there is an intermediate group of farming households such as #14, #27, #36 and #39 that are either tenant farmers, or owner farmers who are tenants as well. Farming is not their only source of income. They own several buildings, and contribute to *kyōgihi* in the range of b ~ h, placing them in the "middle" class. In terms of land ownership within the land readjustment area, #27 comes top, with 0.6 ha, so they are different from the class of landowners with 2 ha or more. However, #14 and #36 clearly own several buildings for residential use. Accordingly it is possible that they can be classed as farming households that obtain a non-farming income from commerce or some other source and also own buildings beyond those needed for

Table 1.3 *Kyōgihi* contributions in Hamada (1939) with details of the number of people paying each amount (residents of Hamada only)

Amount paid (in yen)	Letter of the alphabet used in Table 1.2	No. of people	No. of people whose contribution includes a land tax rate
20 yen and over	a	9	7
10–19 yen	b	10	3
9 yen and over, but less than 10	c	5	1
8 yen and over, but less than 9	d	5	3
7 yen and over, but less than 8	e	6	2
6 yen and over, but less than 7	f	8	2
5 yen and over, but less than 6	g	8	3
4 yen and over, but less than 5	h	7	2
3 yen and over, but less than 4	i	10	3
2 yen and over, but less than 3	j	15	2
1 yen and over, but less than 2	k	24	3
Less than 1 yen	l	43	7
Total		150	38

Source: Ōshōmura Hamada (1939)
Note: *Kyōgihi* are community expenses such as festivals that are not covered by municipal finances

their personal use as a response to urbanization. In other words, ownership of houses (presumably for rent) can be given as a characteristic of farming households in agricultural villages that adjoin cities.

The information in Table 1.2 refers only to farming households in Hamada. Table 1.1 shows landowners in other parts of Ōshō-chūbudaiichi. Of course, Hamada had residents, such as labourers, that did not form farming households; however, with regard to farming households, it is clear that there is a great split between the class of those that own land or buildings, and those that do not.

2.3 *The Implementation of Land Readjustment and Compensation for the Loss of Arable Land*

It can generally be said that the main problem that was experienced during the implementation of land readjustment concerned the relations between owners of tenanted land before readjustment and the tenants who were using the land. In the prewar period, tenant farmers who owned no land could not join land readjustment associations even if they farmed land within the readjustment area. During this period, the normal practice was for landowners to reach agreement about the loss of arable land with such tenant farmers before an association was actually formed, and then prepare it for residential use.[5] This was also the practice in Amagasaki. For example, in the case of the land readjustment project in Tachibana, which was implemented before that of Ōshō-chūbudaiichi, terms of compensation for the loss of arable land were agreed between landowners and tenants in November 1933, just before the association was formed, and the removal of tenants proceeded smoothly (Numajiri 2008).

However, in the case of Ōshō-chūbudaiichi, the land readjustment association acted differently. In June 1939, just before the project began, landowners and tenants agreed compensation of about 1512 yen/ha and this was paid, as will be explained later. Yet information issued by the association indicates that even after the payment of compensation, the tenants continued to farm the land:

(i) A notice to association members from the head of the Ōshō-chūbudaiichi association dated 26 March 1940 shows that cultivation of arable land within the area was continuing because it proclaims that even if crops or irrigation facilities are damaged by the readjustment work, no requests for compensation should be made to the association. Further, the same notice makes it clear that dealings with tenants regarding this issue were entrusted to the landowner involved (KKc).

(ii) It is clear that the work of preparing the reserve land for construction was postponed. The records of the association for 1940 show that it was almost impossible to arrange the funds and materials needed to prepare the land and develop residential sites; further, it was highly unlikely that all the land in the area would be used as residential land even after this work had been completed. Therefore it was proposed that efforts should focus on the provision of roads (Yanagawa-ke). Table 1.4 shows the accounts of income and expenditure for the Ōshō-chūbudaiichi Land Readjustment Association. The columns for annual income show that taken together, in the financial years of 1941 and 1942, sales of reserve land yielded a total income of just over 590,000 yen. But the columns for annual expenditure show that construction work reached a peak in 1941 and showed a steady decline until the end of the war. This was because the wartime economy that came into being immediately after the establishment of the association impeded the construction process. As a result, with the exception of sites that had already been prepared for residential use, cultivation by tenant farmers continued into the postwar period.

[5] *Kukaku Seiri* (Land Readjustment), a prewar magazine, ran a series giving advice on the establishment and management of associations for land readjustment. The process of removing tenants from the land was covered in the very first part of the series, as an essential part of the preparations needed before an association was established (Yokota 1935).

3 Land Readjustment and Arable Land During the Period of Postwar Agricultural Reform

3.1 The Purchase and Sale of Land

A major issue in the implementation of land reform after the end of the war was the question of whether or not to include agricultural land on the outskirts of cities (Ebato 1987). In Amagasaki, too, landowners began a movement opposing the purchase of agricultural land in readjustment areas. In the Tachibana land readjustment area, where the readjustment process had already been completed, resident landlords played a central role. They organised a league to protect residential land in Tachibana and made appeals to the prefecture to designate the area as a zone exempt from purchase based on Clause 4 of Article 5 of the Law Concerning the Special Measures for the Establishment of Owner Farmers (Numajiri 2008). Urbanisation was well under way in the Tachibana readjustment area, and the prefecture did designate it as an exempt zone. It even gave the same treatment to part of the Ōshō-chūbudaiichi readjustment area, even though the development of residential land had been discontinued during the war. The rest of the area was designated as a 5-year suspension of sales zone[6] (Hyōgoken Nōchi kaikaku-shi Hensan Iinkai 1953).

From the viewpoint of tenant farmers, the result was that great differences occurred in the area of land that could be purchased, even within Amagasaki city itself, depending on whether or not the land that they were cultivating was regarded as subject to agricultural land reform. A search of the remaining *Nochi iinkai gijiroku* (Minutes of the agricultural land committee) for farming households in the former Ōshō village that were able to buy farmland in the period July 1948 to February 1950, shows that they were all households situated in its north (AAN 1948–1950). This is clearly linked to the fact that this part of the former village was never included in a land readjustment area. By contrast, since land in the Ōshō-chūbudaiichi readjustment area was either designated as exempt from purchase or subject to a 5-year suspension of sales, none of the farming households there were able to buy land. In Hamada, where agricultural land had been exempted from government purchase, landowner-tenant relationships continued into the post-war period.

[6]The zones were a special measure related to land bought by the government as part of the Agricultural Land Reform Acts. Sales of land in these zones to tenant farmers were postponed for 5 years so that the direction of urbanisation in the zone could be determined.

Table 1.4 Accounts of the Ōshō-chūbudaiichi Land Readjustment Association (Unit: thousand yen)

Year	Income					Expenditure				
		Main items					Main items			
	Total	Sales of reserve land	Loans	Various	Brought forward	Total	Construction costs	Office expenses	Compensation payments	Redemption value
1939	16	—	10	0	—	16	—	8	—	0
1940	90	35	55	0	0	88	75	12	—	1
1941	637	259	350	1	2	515	402	13	27	74
1942	475	332	—	6	122	192	160	13	1	19
1944	587	10	—	16	560	53	36	13	4	—
1945	561	10	—	17	534	32	26	6	—	—
1946	678	140	—	9	530	137	9	68	61	—
1948	1,004	—	—	525	480	527	92	424	10	—
1949	1,035	122	—	435	478	851	140	610	8	—
1950	1,208	750	—	275	184	856	166	675	3	—
1951	1,619	1,077	—	189	353	1,305	330	964	—	—
1952	2,526	2,068	—	145	314	1,842	404	1,438	—	—

Source: Kawabata-ke (KKc)

Note: The accounts for 1943, and 1947 are not known

Total expenditure is the total of the amounts that were actually expended

Because each item has been rounded off to the nearest thousand, the total of "Main items" sometimes exceeds "Total"

Sums remaining have been brought forward as income for the following financial year, but there are cases where the amounts do not tally

3.2 Land Use and the End of Land Readjustment Projects

The Ōshō-chūbudaiichi readjustment association had halted almost all its activities in March 1944, in accordance with a notice issued by the head of the public works department of Hyogo prefecture (KKc). Work continued to stagnate even after the end of the war. It is clear from the accounts of income and expenditure shown in Table 1.4 that expenditure on construction work was not increasing. Likely causes are the actual fall in the value of balances brought forward caused by inflation, and the low possibility of sales of reserve land given the damage brought about by the war. Post-war reports on the project show that by the end of financial year 1951, progress had come to a halt at 60% of completion (KKc).

In contrast to the stagnation of land readjustment projects noted above, during the period of postwar regeneration, there was great interest in the agricultural use of land within the readjustment areas. A good picture of the situation of farming households and arable land in Hamada in the second half of the 1940s can be gained from the diary of Hori Shinji (1914–2002), an owner farmer possessing several houses for rent who had himself found work with the Hanshin Denki Tetsudo (Hanshin Electric Railway) after graduating from middle school (the prewar equivalent of high school in Japan today).

First, there are comments that contrast the hard conditions experienced by salaried employees as a result of postwar inflation, with the income being enjoyed by farmers in Hamada. In an entry for 9 June 1947, for example, Hori Shinji observes that the farming households around him were doing well, with an average daily income of 2000 yen or more, while he was in dire straits since his work at the railway meant that he did not even have enough time to sell the vegetables that he was growing (HS). In an entry for 25 August 1948, he writes that the previous night saw the final performance of the annual Bon-odori celebrations. There was dancing all night in Hamada to the sound of electric gramophones, and some owner farmers had made contributions of as much as 500 yen to the festivities (HS).

In view of the favourable conditions for farming, Hori Shinji himself showed an increased interest in agricultural work. Table 1.5 shows details of the rice-planting activities of the household. From 1939 to 1941, the work was carried out by Hori Shinji's father, other relatives, and people employed for the purpose. Because of his railway duties, Hori himself was not closely involved. But in 1947, partly because of the death of his father,[7] he took time off from work in order to take part. In his diary for the same year, he recorded with satisfaction that he was able to take time off work and complete the rice planting without having to ask any relatives for help (HS 7 July 1947). The next day he added that having taken 5 days off in order to do the rice planting, he felt as if he had retired from the railway, but it had been a positive experience. On the other hand, out of the yearly round of farming events, nothing was as stressful as rice planting (HS 7 July 1947). It is clear that Hori Shinji himself had a positive attitude to farming at this time.

---

[7] Interview with Mr. Hori Kuniomi 4 February 2010.

Second, references to the cultivation of land within readjustment areas also appear quite often in his diaries. From 1948, the Ōshō-chūbudaiichi readjustment association introduced fees for farmers who were cultivating land designated for use as roads. This appears in Table 1.4 as a sharp increase in "various types of income". Hori Shinji was among those who applied to the association's office for permission to cultivate this land (HS 30 September 1948). He also recorded in his diary a decision made by the Hamada council to borrow land from the association to make a communal bed for rice seedlings, and to borrow land from farming household #22 if the association holdings were not sufficient (HS 19 November 1948). In other words, since reserve land owned by the association could not be sold, there was a plan to turn it into communal rice seedling beds instead.

Third, references to conflicts of interest among the landowners, owner farmers and tenants began to appear in the diary. In an entry for 31 May 1948 he wrote that when his wife went to take her turn in guarding the rice seedlings from the sparrows, a member of farming household #18 made a complaint; in addition fun was poked at the Hori family because it was cultivating land designated for use as roads (HS). As is clear from Table 1.2, #18 was a tenant farming household with no outside income that cultivated an area that was relatively large, at least for Hamada. It seems likely that such farming households were critical of households that had alternative sources of income like the Hori family, seeing them as reluctant to participate in activities that were necessary for the village community as a whole. On the other hand, when it was decided that a dry field owned by Hori Shinji would be allocated to another landowner as part of the land readjustment process, Hori complained about the fact that he was going to lose this land in his diary (HS 17 December 1948). He was clearly unhappy about the possibility that arable land that he himself had devoted time to might pass into the ownership of another, more influential, landowner if it was designated for replotting.

While agricultural land in postwar Hamada was not made available for purchase by tenant farmers, their rights of expression within the community increased, along with their income. This was the background against which confrontations over cultivation rights after provisional replotting developed between landowners and tenant farmers in readjustment areas.

4 Confrontations Between Landowners and Tenant Farmers Concerning Provisional Replotting

4.1 The Original Cause of the Problem

In Ōshō-chūbudaiichi, readjustment activities had come to a halt during and immediately after the war. However, on 12 August 1948, the association made an announcement concerning the designation of some of the land that was to be readjusted, with effect from 15 November of the same year. In response, landowners

Table 1.5 Changes in the source of labour for rice planting as shown in Hori Shinji's diary

Year	Dates of rice planting	Identity of labourers	What Hori himself was doing
1939	2–4 July	Father, mother, Hori himself, his younger brother and sister, 2 hired labourers	Worked at the railway every day, but helped early in the morning, etc.
1940	3–5 July	Father, mother, hired labour	Worked at the railway every day
1941	6–8 July	Father, mother, Hori himself, his younger sister	On 6 July, worked at the railway, but returned home at 15:55 and then helped. Helped on the 7th as it was a public holiday
1947	3–5 July	Mother, Hori himself, his wife, younger brother and sister. (An aunt was asked to look after the child/children.)	Took leave from work so that he could spend all his time rice planting
1948	3–4 July	Hori himself, his wife, younger sister and brother, two members of an aunt's family and 4 hired labourers	Took leave from work so that he could spend all his time rice planting
1951	3–4 July	Hori himself, his wife, younger sister and brother, two neighbours, hired labour	Took leave from work so that he could spend all his time rice planting
1952	2–4 July	Hori's wife, his younger sister, hired labour	Worked at the railway every day, with night duty on the 3rd

Source: HS (1939–1941, 1947–1948, 1951–1952)
Note: The identity of the labourers is as given in the source

who were affected asked the tenants who were cultivating the land to leave and move to their provisionally replotted land before readjustment took place. This provoked strong opposition from the tenant farmers and in March of the following year (1949), tenant farmer #1 (see Table 1.2) and 12 other farmers presented a petition to the Amagasaki City Agricultural Land Committee (AAN 1949).

The petition cited four examples of the effect on individual tenant farmers. They can be summarized as follows:

(i) The case of tenant farmer #42,[8] who had been asked to vacate the land he was farming now (0.1 ha) and move to provisionally replotted land of only 0.06 ha;
(ii) The case of tenant farmer #9, who had lost part of the land he was farming now (0.1 ha) to another landowner because of provisional replotting and was being asked to vacate that part by the new landowner;
(iii) The case of tenant farmer #12, whose landowner had lost land as a result of temporary relocation. He had been asked to split his parcel of tenanted land (0.1 ha) and cultivate only one part of it;
(iv) The case of tenant farmer #43, who had been asked by the landowner to vacate his 0.05 ha of tenanted land for the reasons already given in cases (ii) and (iii).

[8] When the relationship between the household of this farmer and the farming households in Table 1.2 was not clear, numbers #42 and above have been assigned for reasons of expediency.

The tenant farmers used these examples as reasons for being allowed to continue to use the arable land that they had been cultivating before provisional replotting.

Two of the farming households mentioned above, #9 and #12, can be identified in Table 1.2. Household #9 depended completely on farming for its income, having the tenancy of a total of 0.4 ha of arable land. Its class in terms of *kyōgihi* contributions was k. Household #12 depended mainly on farming for its income, having the tenancy of a total of 0.6 ha, and a class of g in terms of *kyōgihi* contributions. Household #1, which also played a role in the petition, depended mainly on farming for its income and had a class of k in terms of *kyōgihi* contributions. #1 and #9 were not members of the Ōshō-chūbudaiichi Land Readjustment Association, but #12 was.

Tenant farmers who did not have land or buildings in Hamada joined tenant farmers who were association members in presenting the petition. As has already been stated, none of the tenant farmers who lived in Hamada had been given the chance to buy agricultural land as a result of land reform. With reference to the possibility that they might experience a reduction in the area of land that they were able to cultivate as part of land readjustment, the tenant farmers additionally asked the Agricultural Land Committee to affirm their present cultivation rights. The arguments of the farmers are said to have their roots in the preliminary responses of staff in the Hyogo prefecture agricultural division and the Kyoto agricultural affairs bureau of the Ministry of Agriculture and Forestry, who had stated that there was no need to move cultivation rights when land was provisionally replotted (KKc). In other words, the tenant farmers argued that they should be able to continue cultivation of the land that they had been cultivating before provisional replotting on the basis of Article 8 of the Farmland Adjustment Law, which prescribed the validity of the leasing of agricultural land with regard to third parties.

At a meeting held on 15 March 1949, the Amagasaki City Agricultural Land Committee initially accepted the arguments of the tenant farmers. However, the Ōshō-chūbudaiichi Land Readjustment Association and some of the landowners presented a separate appeal to the Committee in order to justify their stance. The arguments of the Association were as follows (AAN 1949):

First, the Association considered that once provisional replotting had been decided, cultivation rights should be moved to the actual parcel of land that had been designated according to the replotting. In support of this view it cited the query dated 5 June 1948 made by the governor of Aichi prefecture to the head of the City Bureau of the Ministry of Construction and the reply of the head of the City Bureau. The governor's question was "When the actual site and area (land parcel) of cultivation rights have been changed through replotting resulting from land readjustment, is it correct to assume that this means that farming activities should be moved to the land designated by the readjustment?" and the City Bureau's reply was "That is the case. This is what has been agreed with the Ministry of Agriculture and Forestry (AAN 1949)." In other words, they justified their interpretation of the rights of landowners vis-à-vis tenants by drawing attention to the policy of the Ministry of Construction.

Second, the Association also challenged the actual cultivation rights of tenant farmers. Since tenant farmers in the Ōshō-chūbudaiichi land readjustment area had been paid compensation for the loss of their land in 1939, they claimed that this land no longer had any recognised cultivators (AAN 1949). However, even the Association did not consider that the payment of compensation in 1939 of itself meant that the landowner-tenant relationship no longer existed at the end of the war. Cultivation had continued in most tenanted land even after 1939, and the peasants had made payments of some kind to the landlords in recognition of the fact that they had been able to harvest the land. Land designated for use as roads had also been cultivated by tenants because construction work had not started. Where this happened, landowners and representatives of tenants had agreed that the half the tenancy fee would be paid in financial year 1949 and that there would be no fees payable from financial year 1950 until construction work began (AAN 1949). In other words, the association emphasized that although compensation for the loss of land had been paid in 1939, tenant farmers had continued to be able to harvest the land. This being the case, it was completely unreasonable of the tenant farmers to expect to be able to retain the arable land that they had cultivated before land relocation (AAN 1949).

The Amagasaki City Agricultural Land Committee discussed the association's appeal at a meeting held on 2 April 1949. As a result, it resolved to withdraw its acceptance of the tenant farmer's petition. Instead, it proposed first, that if the area of a tenant's arable land was decreased as a result of land adjustment, the cultivation rights that were given should be proportionate to the original area, and second, that the association, the cultivators, and the landowners should meet and strive together to arrive at a solution that would satisfy everyone (AAN 1949). In this way, the problem was once more returned for discussion by the association (the landowners) and the tenant farmers.

4.2 *The Discussions Between the Landowners and the Tenant Farmers*

As a result, four local members of the Amagasaki City Agricultural Land Committee arranged an informal meeting for 7 April 1949 so that people involved in the association and tenant farmer representatives could exchange views. At this meeting, the committee members made their own suggestion. They proposed that if replotted land was designated for educational or police use, tenants should be able to cultivate this land for no charge until the construction of the public facilities began. However, the tenant farmers refused to accept this, and the attempt at reconciliation failed (KKc). The next month, a new petition calling for the purchase by the government of agricultural land in the readjustment area was presented to the Agricultural Land Committee. The petition contained the signatures of 23 farming households led by household #18 and stated that in the light of the present situation regarding agricultural land, the signatories could not accept any proposals to suspend sales for 5 years

(AAN 1949). Since the signatories were tenant farmers of Hamada, where almost all the land had either been exempted from purchase (or had been subject to a 5-year suspension of sales), it seems reasonable to interpret this second petition as motivated by a strong desire among the tenant farmers to actually become owners of land.

On 18 June, just before rice planting began, the Agricultural Land Committee representatives suggested a second compromise solution that accepted the concept of provisional replotting. In addition to accepting the free cultivation of land designated for public use until construction began, it proposed that decreases in land area as a result of readjustment should be held at an average of 40%, and that while tenant farmers should move to provisionally replotted land, they should be able to retain as arable land 60% of the area that they had farmed previously (KKc). Because this solution contained the possibility that the landowners would have to accept point iii of the petition presented by the tenant farmers to the Agricultural Land Committee on 15 March, the initial response of the association was negative, but eventually it indicated a willingness to agree.

Meanwhile, the tenant farmers took this second compromise solution into consideration and on 28 June presented the following two demands to the Agricultural Land Committee and the association as conditions for agreeing to move to the provisionally replotted land (KKc):

(i) compensation of 302.5 yen/m^2 for each metre of land that they would lose;
(ii) alternatively, free ownership rights to half of all replotted land, plus recognition of their cultivation rights over the remaining half and permission to continue cultivating it.

The conditions presented by the tenant farmers on the 28th were based on the premise that they would accept the move to the provisionally replotted land. In that sense, they had made a concession, since up till now they had demanded to be allowed to continue cultivating the land that they had used before land readjustment took place. However, closer examination reveals that at 302.5 yen/m^2, the compensation for land loss that they were seeking was far higher than any of the three examples of compensation paid to tenant farmers in Amagasaki that can be ascertained. These all date from 1951 and ranged from 54 to 67 yen/m^2 (AAN 1951; AN 1951). In fact, the price that they were asking for was equivalent to that being paid for residential land.[9] Moreover, even if they lost an average of 40% of their allotted parcel area because of the government policy of agricultural land reduction, since they were demanding ownership rights to half of the remaining 60% (30% of their area of cultivated land before replotting), their alternative proposal merely substituted the loss of land for a gain in ownership rights. Given that the sales price of ownership of agricultural land in Amagasaki at the time was 66–91 yen/m^2 (AAN 1950–1951), the alternative proposal did not necessarily mean a loss in assets on the tenants' side. In fact, it was a plan that would certainly give them the ownership rights that they so wanted.

[9] According to a survey of September 1954, the lowest price for dealings in residential land in the city of Kōbe in Hyōgo prefecture was 302.5 yen (Kensetsushō Jūtakukyoku 1954).

The prefectural farmland official in charge of tenancy issues concluded that the tenants were not interested in looking for a peaceful solution to the issue (KKc). The association reacted similarly, and announced that it was breaking off its negotiations. A few days later, on 1 July, with rice planting about to start, it applied to the Kōbe District Court for a provisional injunction that would keep the tenants off the land that they intended to plant. The injunction was immediately granted (KKc). Formal tenancy arbitration procedures began in September 1949, but when they were broken off in June the next year it became clear that the dispute would take a long time to settle.

4.3 The Responses of Central Government Ministries and Agencies and the Amagasaki City Agricultural Land Committee

Part of the problem was the fact that the Ministry of Agriculture and Forestry did not have a clear policy regarding problems related to land adjustment and cultivation rights. In 1948, the head of the Kyoto Agricultural Land Affairs Bureau asked the head of the Agricultural Land Division of the Ministry for information about the relationship between Article 8 of the Farmland Adjustment Law and Article 17 of the Arable Land Readjustment Law. On 20 December, the Division head replied that leasing rights would be transferred to land after it had been relocated (Nōchi Kaikaku Shiryō Hensan Iinkai 1981, pp. 684–685). The very fact that such questions and answers were being exchanged at the end of 1948 surely reveals that no advance preparations were being made to deal with the type of dispute that might be expected to occur regarding the relationship between cultivation rights, as set out in the Farmland Adjustment Law, and the replotting that would accompany land readjustment, as set out in the Arable Land Readjustment Law.

Moreover, this reply from the Ministry of Agriculture and Forestry was not fully absorbed by the Kyoto Agricultural Land Affairs Bureau. The tenant farmers had adopted such an unyielding stance in negotiations that on 25 June 1949, the Ōshōchūbudaiichi Land Readjustment Association visited the Bureau in Kyoto. There they discovered that the arguments of the tenant side were based on the interpretation of a Bureau official that cultivation rights did not belong to the person who owned the land but to the land itself, and that this was why the tenants held that the replotting of land did not require them to move from the land that they were already cultivating. The association members were apparently astonished that a Bureau official could hand down such an extreme and defective interpretation of the Farmland Adjustment Law (KKc).

By contrast, the Amagasaki City Agricultural Land Committee was very cautious in giving judgements related to cultivation rights in land readjustment areas. Within the Committee there was a group, mainly composed of members who were tenant farmers, that urged the protection of those who were actually cultivating the land in

Hamada. At a meeting of 21 April 1949, the point was made that committee decisions must be based on the Farmland Adjustment Law, which was exactly the same as the argument made by the official in the Kyoto Agricultural Land Affairs Bureau (AAN 1949). Committee members also criticised the standards that were being used to exempt areas from purchase as agricultural land under Clause 4, Article 5 of the Law Concerning the Special Measures for the Establishment of Owner Farmers and pointed to unfair profits being made by particular landowners, or particular tenant farmers (AAN 1949). In other words, the Agricultural Land Committee was to a certain extent aware of the various issues involving cultivation rights with regard to the temporary relocation of land.

Yet its awareness of these issues did not lead it to present standards or models that would support the tenant farmers' demands for cultivation without any modifications. As has already been pointed out, during the period from March to April 1949 when both the tenant farmers and the association (the landowners) were making petitions and appeals, the Agricultural Land Committee made no decisions itself, but urged the parties involved to find a solution. One reason why it avoided making a decision was the argument of one of the landowner representatives, Kawabata Mataichi, that the Committee did not have the authority to state that there was no need for tenant farmers to move the location of their cultivated land even after provisional replotting (AAN 1949).[10] In any case, the Agricultural Land Committee avoided making any decision regarding the location of cultivation rights when land was provisionally replotted.

5 Tenant Farmers and the Settlement of the Issue of Provisional Replotting

5.1 The Tenant Farmers' Acceptance of Provisionally Replotted Land

It was only from the end of 1950 that any change began in the confrontation between the two groups. In November 1950, judgement was given against the tenant farmers in the litigation calling for an end to the 5-year suspension of sales zones that they had lodged against the governor of Hyogo (KKc). Then in February 1951, representatives of the tenants expressed their earnest desire to settle the dispute since the changing social situation had led them to recognise the need for more residential land. On 25 June, all those involved met at the main hall of the temple of Jōsenji in Hamada to sign a compromise agreement (KKc). The content itself is not clear, but there seems to be little doubt that it was based on the unofficial plan of the Agricultural Land Committee, which accepted the provisional replotting of land. The grounds for this conclusion are the fact that it was the tenants who had asked

[10] Kawabata Mataichi was a central figure in the Tachibana League for Protecting Residential Land that was mentioned in 3.1 (Numajiri 2008).

for settlement of the dispute, the fact that there are no references in the association records to losses by the association or payments of compensation, and finally the reissuing of the notice about the designation of sites planned for replotting in 5-year suspension of sales zones in Hamada on 26 June, the day after the signing of the agreement (KKc). The reason for the tenant farmers' sudden change in attitude is also not clear. However, it can be inferred that the defeat of their litigation against the prefectural governor in November 1950 and the renewed movement toward urbanisation in the district shown by the construction of an elementary school (see later) meant that their only path was to accept provisionally replotted land. As a result, the tenant farmers had gained in the sense that they had received compensation for loss of land and yet had been able to keep farming until provisional replotting took place; on the other hand, they had been forced to move to smaller parcels of land as a result of the replotting.

Following provisional replotting, land for public use was secured in Hamada for facilities including an elementary school, a police station, and a park. The need for an elementary school was particularly urgent due to the rapid increase in population after the war years. It was opened in the June 1951, the very month in which the landowners and tenant farmers had signed their agreement (Amagasakishi-ritsu Hamada shōgakkō Sōritsu 50 shūnen kinen-shi bukai 2000). In this way, the project was able to encourage urban formation by realising part of its initial plan for obtaining land for public use by reducing the area of arable land.

Meanwhile, however, as Table 1.4 shows, inflation and the stagnating sales of reserve land meant that construction projects such as the provision of roads, were at a standstill, just as they had been at the end of the war. In 1956, when the registration of readjusted land was completed, the association had only achieved 67% of its goals. It disbanded that year, leaving the remaining work to be done by the city (KKc). The land readjustment projects had relied on the idea that land prices would rise when agricultural land was turned into residential land and that the price rises would provide enough funds for the readjustment to be carried out by non-government organisations. However, the initial plans had not been fully realised.

5.2 Occasional Work by Tenant Farmers

To investigate the activities of tenant farmers and changes in agricultural labour around the time of the 1951 agreement between landowners and tenant farmers, it is possible to turn once again to Hori Shinji's diaries. With regard to Hori Shinji himself, 1951 signalled a retreat from involvement in agricultural work. As Table 1.5 shows, he took part in rice planting but took only 3 days off work, and in the next year he took no days off, but performed his railway duties throughout. After his father's death during the war, Hori Shinji had shared the burden of farm work at busy periods in the second half of the 1940s, but in the 1950s he once again began to adopt a more negative attitude.

Important here is the fact that from around this time, Hori Shinji began to rely on tenant farming household #1 to perform activities such as the cultivation of his land in preparation for rice planting. In 1951, he also left the cultivation of his land after the rice harvest to the same household. In other words, the Hori family itself performed tasks such as rice planting and harvesting, but left the heavy work of rice field cultivation to tenant farmers working on an occasional basis. In his diary entry for 18 June 1951, when he made the request to household #1, he estimated that it would cost about 10,000 yen (HS); when the family came to collect their pay, however, he recorded his relief that their charges were relatively low (HS 6 July 1951). This suggests that the cost of occasional work was rising and that the expense worried him. Before the rice planting that year, he had written in the diary that he felt crushed by the competing demands of family and workplace (HS 13 June 1951). However, in 1952 he noted that recently he felt as if he completely belonged to the railway company, and that he no longer went to view his rice fields of his own accord (HS 13 September 1952). This suggests that his interest in agricultural labour was waning because of the demands of his salaried work. Since most of the farming households in Hamada had non-agricultural sources of income, it is likely that one cause of the rise in the cost of occasional work was the fact that other owner farming households were turning to it, for reasons similar to Hori Shinji's. Household #1 had been one of the representatives of the tenant farmers when they were pursuing the issue of provisional replotting. The area of land that it cultivated had been greatly reduced after the war, as will be explained in detail below. It is likely that occasional work was an important source of cash income for tenant farming households that had lost a lot of land in this way.

Entries in Hori Shinji's diaries for the period following the settlement of the provisional replotting issue show that tenant farmers were closely involved in running village affairs. For example, household #18 requested Hori Shinji's help in repairing the sluice gates (HS 15 October 1951) and also asked him to take part in the election for the water resources committee (HS 23 June 1952). In other words, although they had not benefitted from the agricultural reform programme, the tenant farmers had continued to farm and had also improved their social position within the area.

5.3 *Tenant Farmers' Demands Regarding the Remaining Arable Land*

What happened to the agricultural land in Hamada after provisional replotting? The many changes that occurred from the second half of the 1950s onwards cannot be dealt with here. However, it is worth pointing out that in the first half of the decade there were some tenant farmers who wished to maintain and even expand their arable land after provisional replotting. In August 1953, four farming households, including #1, #4, and #20, applied to the Amagasaki City Agricultural Committee for permission to lease nationally owned agricultural land in the Ōshō-chūbudaiichi land readjustment area. #1 was applying for the lease of 0.04 ha, #4 was applying for 0.12 ha, #20 for 0.1 ha, and the final household for 0.14 ha. As Table 1.2 shows,

#20 was a large scale owner farmer in Hamada, but #1 and #4 were tenant households. #1 was the household that had undertaken occasional work for the Hori family. In 1938 it cultivated a total of 0.74 ha of land, all as tenancies (Table 1.2), but the application for nationally owned land reveals that in 1953 it was only cultivating 0.36 ha, still all as tenancies (AN 1953). This nationally owned land was land that had not been sold because of the 5 year suspension of sales stipulated in the regulations for the implementation of the Law concerning Special Measures for the Establishment of Owner Farmers,[11] but the tenant farmers had applied for leases on the grounds that there were no provisions for the suspension of sales in the Agricultural Land Act.

The Committee's initial response to these applications was to postpone any deliberations because there was an ongoing dispute with a third party regarding the land in question (AN 1953). At the next meeting of the Committee, in September, members were told that the four applicants were the present cultivators of the land for which they were applying; that they were people who should have moved as a result of provisional replotting, in other words that they were the cultivators of this land before the relocation process; that by chance, there had been no designated cultivator of these lots at the time of relocation; and that since the land had not had any cultivators since the relocation process the four had continued to cultivate it and therefore wished to apply for leases. In response, it was suggested that if the present cultivators were considered to be suitable candidates, leases should be agreed, and this is what the Committee decided (AN 1953). In other words, the Committee recognised that in the case of land subject to a 5-year suspension of sales, if the tenant farmer from before provisional replotting had continued to cultivate it without moving even after replotting, applications for leasing should be agreed.

In July of the next year, further applications for leases of nationally held agricultural land in the Ōshō-chūbudaiichi land readjustment area were made by farming households #12 and #18. These were also approved (AN 1954). That April, households #1 and #12, which were both interested in leasing, had also obtained ownership of part of their tenanted land (0.12 and 0.1 ha respectively) when ownership rights were transferred from the landowner in accordance with Article 3 of the Agricultural Land Act (AN 1954). It is therefore clear that even after provisional replotting, tenant farmers continued to support the cultivation of arable land.

On the other hand, at a meeting of the City Agricultural Committee in August 1953, there was an application from the Mayor of Amagasaki for the grounds of Hamada Elementary School to be extended by changing the use of 0.36 ha of the surrounding agricultural land according to Article 5 of the Agricultural Land Act. The estimated price of the land was given at 605 yen/m^2 (AN 1953). Examination of the minutes of the Agricultural Land (Agricultural) Committee shows no example of tenant farmers trying to turn their land into residential sites in this way. Although at this stage it cannot be said that there was any expansion in the class of farming households that owned several buildings beyond those such as #14, #27, #36 and

[11] For the historical background to the formation of nationally held agricultural land, see Tachibana (1971).

#39 that were mentioned earlier, it is important to note that in Hamada in the first part of the 1950s, there were new indications of urbanisation in the form of both applications to change agricultural use and rising land prices.

6 Conclusion

The purpose of this section is to give a final overview of the conflict of interests between landowners and tenant farmers that accompanied the Ōshō-chūbudaiichi land readjustment project and the process by which the conflict was brought to an end. In addition, it will outline both the special features of urban formation that occurred as a result of the situation in this district and the role of the tenant farmers who were the actual cultivators of the land.

With regard to the arable land in the readjustment area during the wartime period when the project began, the following two points can be made concerning the nature of the compensation offered by the landowners and the actual cultivating activities of the tenant farmers:

(i) Although peasant cultivation rights were strengthened during the war, laws and regulations concerning city planning were not revised to take this into account. As a result, landowners tried to compensate tenant farmers financially for the loss of land before the readjustment project began, as had been the practice up to the mid-1930s.
(ii) Since the project experienced delays as a result of the nature of the wartime economy and the attempt to turn arable land into residential land was postponed, cultivation by tenant farmers in the area continued until after the end of the war.

As a result, during the period of postwar reforms, there was a direct conflict of interests between the landowners, who wanted to revive their previous land readjustment activities, and tenant farmers, who wanted to continue to farm the land. From the landowners' point of view, tenant farmers had already been compensated for any loss of land. This was because as well as receiving financial compensation in the form of land-loss payments before the readjustment project began, they had also continued to receive the benefit of being able to continue to cultivate the land even after readjustment had started. They used the notification sent by the Ministry of Construction to justify their assumption that the cultivation rights of tenant farmers should be transferred to the reduced land areas that they were granted after the process of provisional replotting. On the other hand, tenant farmers were aware that in legal terms their position had been strengthened by the Agricultural Land Reform Acts and that in financial terms, farming households on the outskirts of cities were in an advantageous situation. This had strengthened their sense of ownership regarding the land that they had continued to cultivate as tenants during the war, even though it had already been designated for readjustment. Even after provisional replotting, they petitioned the Amagasaki City Agricultural Land Committee for permission to continue cultivating the same areas of arable land as before readjustment. However, the demands of the tenant farmers were not limited to the cultivation of land. During their negotiations with landowners, they demanded sums in compensation that far exceeded the market in land-loss payments of the time. In other words, while tenant farmers were emphasising their right to continue cultivating activities, they were also aware of the rise in land prices that followed the conversion of agricultural land into residential land, which was, of course, the premise that made land readjustment viable.

The conflict between landowners and tenant farmers continued for some time, but after losing their litigation seeking the cancellation of the 5-year suspension of sales zones, the tenant farmers were willing to reach a settlement with the landowners. In this sense, the conflict over provisional replotting ended in acceptance of the view of the landowners, who followed the policies of the government as represented by the Ministry of Construction and the Ministry of Agriculture and Forestry. Yet to understand what was happening, it is necessary to pay note to the efforts of the tenant farmers to justify their stance by using the Amagasaki City Agricultural Land Committee as an intermediary, for example when they presented it with a petition. As will be explained later, this is because their activities influenced the way in which urban formation was to develop.

This chapter has focussed on a case study of conflicts between the land readjustment project and the way in which peasants were using the land. The features of urban formation that have been revealed through this case study can be summed up as follows:

(i) The opening up of land for public use was made possible by the provisional replotting of land in accordance with the claims of landowners. But it is necessary to note the following two points. First, land readjustment proceeded without fully taking into account the opinions of the tenant farmers, who could not join land readjustment associations. Second, aspects of land readjustment such as road provision were not able to proceed smoothly because of the reduction in income caused by inflation and the stagnation in sales of reserved land. These points can be said to show the limits of what land readjustment could achieve under the leadership of landowners.[12]

(ii) There were cases in which agricultural land continued to exist in land readjustment areas. This occurred because some tenant farmers made efforts to maintain their agricultural activities on privately owned land, particularly when there was a large amount of agricultural land in the readjustment area. They did so by performing occasional work for landowners and influential farmers, and by cultivating arable land where there was no cultivator after provisional replotting had taken place. Of great importance here is the fact that both tenant and owner

[12] In view of the fact that the yield on residential land for rent in the neighbouring Tachibana readjustment area was showing a downturn (Numajiri 2009), it is likely that the income of landowners in the Ōshō-chūbudaiichi land readjustment area from letting land and housing was also going down. The Rent Control Act and the general strengthening of the rights of tenants of rental housing were among the causes.

farmers developed ways of getting City Agricultural Land Committees (Agricultural Committees) to recognise their use of land within readjustment areas as agricultural land, and even the expansion of their holdings, by giving evidence of their ability to cultivate and the results of their cultivation efforts. One example of these ways can be seen in applications for leases of nationally owned agricultural land. There was a wide gap between the 1919 City Planning Act that served as a model for land readjustment by associations, and the system laid down by the Agricultural Land Reform Acts, on which tenant farmers relied. At the time, those who were in charge of city planning tended to see this agricultural legislation in a negative light.[13] But in fact, tenant farmers continued to cultivate land in readjustment areas even after provisional replotting, and because Agricultural Land Committees (Agricultural Committees) recognised this, agricultural land use became an integral part of the urban formation of land readjustment areas even though it was a use of land that had not been given a positive role in the original plans for urban formation.

From the early 1950s, signs of urbanisation appeared once more in Hamada; in the following period of rapid economic growth, there was an obvious rise in the proportion of residential land. What effect did this have on the behavior of tenant and owner farmers who wished to go on using agricultural land?[14] Was there an increase in the number of farming households with other sources of income? Households of this type, whose positive response to urbanisation is suggested by the number of buildings that they owned, had existed in Hamada since before the war. Examination of changes in land use during Japan's period of rapid economic growth is the next topic that needs to be considered by those working in this field.

Postscript

After writing this article, the author produced a book (Numajiri 2015) that contained enlarged and corrected versions of this and other articles, including Numajiri (2008, 2009). The book included an attempt to analyse changes in land use during Japan's period of rapid economic growth, the topic that was mentioned above. Those interested should consult the volume. Further, the book used historical documents related to Hamada that were discovered after the writing of this article. These materials led to changes in the author's view that are explained below:

---

[13] Ishihara Kōsaku, a technical official at the Ministry of Construction, stated that from the city planning side, great problems were caused by the fact that land in readjustment areas under the City Planning Act and green areas designated for parks were considered as targets of agricultural reform and were even sold to owner farmers or made into areas where sales were suspended for five years (Ishihara 1957).

[14] In January 1955, tenant farmers from Hamada also applied to buy nationally owned agricultural land (land that had previously been subject to a five year postponement of sales) on the basis of Article 36 of the Agricultural Land Act (AN 1955).

(i) A copy of the decision regarding the litigation of November 1950 was discovered. (It is owned by an individual but has been lent to the Amagasaki Municipal Archives.) From this it is clear that since the designation of 5-year suspension of sales zones was not within the power of administrative disposition, the prefecture suggested that municipally run Agricultural Land Committees could make proposals regarding plans to sell land in such areas. The court supported this view. Moreover, it is also clear that tenant farmers asked for permission to buy nationally owned land before any judgement was made regarding their litigation. This suggests that they were using the prefecture's view of the matter as a counterattack to strengthen their arguments in favour of buying land. (For evidence with regard to this last point, see also AAN 1950.)

(ii) It was also discovered that at the December 1958 meeting of the Amagasaki Agricultural Committee, permission had actually been given for the transfer of rights over rice fields in Hamada on the basis of Article 3 of the Agricultural Land Law (AN 1958). The transfer of rights was justified as compensation for the loss of land as a result of land readjustment, and it was explained at the meeting that it was a condition necessary for the settlement of a dispute concerning land readjustment. As a result, in Numajiri (2015), the interpretation of the nature of the agreement made between landowners and tenant farmers was changed in order to show that it was possible for tenant farmers to receive compensation for the loss of land.

References

Amagasaki Nōgyō Iinkai (AN). 1951, 1953–1955, 1958. *Amagasaki Nōgyō Iinkai Gijiroku* [Minutes of the Amagasaki Agricultural Committee], (Amagasaki City Agricultural Committee).

Amagasakishi-ritsu Hamada Shōgakkō Sōritsu 50-shūnen Kinen-shi Bukai, ed. 2000. *Amagasaki shi-ritsu Hamada Shōgakkō sōritsu 50-shunen kinen-shi* [History of the first 50 years of Hamada Elementary School]. Amagasaki: Amagasakishi-ritsu Hamada Shōgakkō Sōritsu 50-shūnen Kinen Jigyō Jikkō Iinkai.

Amagasakishi Amagasaki-chiku Nōchi Iinkai (AAN). 1948–1951. *Amagasakishi Amagasaki-chiku Nōchi Iinkai Gijiroku* [Minutes of the Amagasaki City Agricultural Land Committee], (Amagasaki City Agricultural Committee).

Amagasakishi Toshikyoku Keikakubu Toshikeikakuka, ed. 1992. *Amagasaki no toshikeikaku* [City Planning in Amagasaki]. Amagasaki: Amagasakishi Toshikyoku Keikakubu Toshikeikakuka.

Ebato, Akira. 1987. *Tokyo no chiiki kenkyū* [Area Studies of Tokyo]. Tokyo: Daimeidō.

Enomoto, Kakurō, ed. 1942. *Ōshōson-shi* [Chronicles of Ōshō]. Amagasaki: Ōshōmura Kyōiku Chōsakai.

Harada, Sumitaka, ed. 2001. *Nihon no toshihō* [Urban Laws of Japan], vol. 1. Tokyo: Tokyo Daigaku Shuppankai.

Hori, Shinji (HS). 1939–1941, 1947–1948, 1951–1952. *Hori Shinji Nikki* [Diaries of HORI Shinji], (In private ownership).

Hyōgoken Nōchi Kaikaku-shi Hensan Iinkai, ed. 1953. *Hyōgoken nōchi kaikaku-shi* [A History of Agricultural Land Reforms in Hyogo Prefecture. Kobe: Hyōgoken Nōchirinmubu Nōchi Kaitakuka.

Ishida, Yorifusa. 2004. *Nihon kingendai toshi keikaku no tenkai 1868–2003* [The Development of City Planning in Modern Japan, 1868–2003]. Tokyo: Jichitai Kenkyūsha.
Ishihara, Kōsaku. 1957. Sengo 10nen no kaiko to kongo heno kibō [A Review of the Period 1945 to 1955 and Prospects for the Future]. *Shin Toshi* (New Cities) 11 (1).
Iwami, Ryōtarō. 1978. *Tochi kukaku seiri no kenkyū* [Studies in Land Readjustment]. Tokyo: Jichitai Kenkyūsha.
Kawabata-ke (KKa). 1933–1944. *Tachibana Kukaku Seiri Shorui Tsuzuri* [File of Documents Related to Land Readjustment in Tachibana], (Amagasaki Municipal Archives, KAWABATA Masakazu Papers (2): 628).
Kawabata-ke (KKb). 1938–1951. *Tachibana-daini Tochi kukaku seiri kumiai Shorui Tsuzuri* [File of Documents Related to the Tachibana-daini Land Readjustment Association), (Amagasaki Municipal Archives, KAWABATA Masakazu Papers (2): 630).
Kawabata-ke (KKc). 1939–1957. *Ōshōmura Chūbu-daiichi Tochi Kukaku Seiri Kumiai Shorui Tsuzuri* [File of Documents Related to the Ōshōmura Chūbu-daiichi Land Readjustment Association], (Amagasaki Municipal Archives, KAWABATA Masakazu Papers (2): 631).
Kensetsushō Jūtakukyoku, ed. 1954. *Tochi oyobi jūtaku kakaku chōsa kekka hōkokusho* [A Report on the Results of a Survey into the Prices of Land and Housing]. Tokyo: Kensetsushō Jūtakukyoku.
Koshizawa, Akira. 1991. *Tokyo no toshi keikaku* [City Planning in Tokyo]. Tokyo: Iwanami Shoten.
Nōchi Kaikaku Shiryō Hensan Iinkai, ed. 1981. *Nōchi kaikaku shiryō shūsei* [Collected Materials Related to Agricultural Land Reforms], vol.15. Tokyo: Ochanomizu Shobō.
Nōsei Chōsakai, ed. 1956. *Nōchi kaikaku jiken kiroku* [Records of Incidents Related to Land Reform]. Tokyo: Nōsei Chōsakai.
Numajiri, Akinobu. 2002. *Kōjō ritchi to toshi keikaku* [Plant Location and City Planning]. Tokyo: Tokyo Daigaku Shuppankai.
———. 2008. 1930-nendai no nōson ni okeru shigaichi keisei to jinushi [Urban Formation and Landowners in Rural Communities in the 1930s]. *Rekishi to Keizai* [The Journal of Political Economy and Economic History] 200.
———. 2009. Tochi kukaku seirigo no shigaichi keisei ni kansuru ichikōsatsu [A Study of Urban Formation After Land Readjustment]. In *Dai 6-kai Higashi Ajia keizaishi shinpojiumu: Higashi Ajia ni okeru keizai hatten no hikaku* [The 6th Symposium on the Economic History of East Asia]. Tokyo: Gendai Nihon Keizaishi Kenkyūkai, and Sangyōshi Kenkyūkai.
———. 2015. *Sonraku kara mita shigaichi keisei* [The Process of Urban Formation as Seen from Rural Communities]. Tokyo: Nihon Keizai Hyōronsha.
Ōishi, Kaichirō and Kanazawa, Fumio, eds. 2003. *Kindai Nihon toshi-shi kenkyū* [Studies in the History of the City in Modern Japan]. Tokyo: Nihon Keizai Hyōronsha.
Okazaki, Sōtarō. 1925. *Toshi keikaku to hōsei* [City Planning and the Legal System]. Tokyo: Kinkōdō Shoseki.
Ōshō-chūbu daiichi Tochi Kukaku Seiri Kumiai. *Kumiaiin no Shimei narabini sono Shoyū suru Tochi no Chiseki Chintai Kakaku* [Names of Association Members and the Price of the Land Parcel that they Own], (Amagasaki Municipal Archives, MORI Genitsu Papers 2 (3): 38).
Ōshōmura Hamada. 1939–1942. *Kyōgihi Chōshū Daichō* [Register of *Kyōgihi* Contributions], (Amagasaki Municipal Archives, Hamada Buraku Papers, 100).
Ōshōmura Yakuba (ŌYa). 1938. *Nōka Chōsa Shorui* (Documents Related to Agricultural Surveys), (Amagasaki Municipal Archives).
Ōshōmura Yakuba (ŌYb). 1934. *Hyōgoken Mukogun Ōshōmura Kaokuzei Fukagakuhyō* [Table of Amounts Levied in Buildings Tax in Muko, Ōshōmura, Hyogo Prefecture], (Amagasaki Municipal Archives, YANAGAWA Keiichi Papers (2): 825–4).
Suzuki, Yūichirō. 2004. *Kindai Nihon no daitoshi keisei* [The Formation of Large Cities in Modern Japan]. Tokyo: Iwata Shoin.
Tachibana, Takeo. 1971. *Kokuyū nōchi no urimodoshi mondai ni tsuite* [On the Resale of Nationally Owned Agricultural Land]. *Reference* 243.

Takashima, Shūichi. 2003. *Senkan-ki toshi kinkō ni okeru tochi seiri to chiiki shakai* [Changes in Tokyo Suburbs Due to the Land Readjustment Projects of the 1920s to 1930s]. *Rekishi to Keizai* [The Journal of Political Economy and Economic History] 180.

———. 2004. *Senkan-ki toshi kinko ni okeru toshi kaihatsu to tochi seiri* [Urban Development and Land Readjustment in the Interwar Tokyo Suburbs]. *Shakai Keizai Shigaku* (Socio-economic History) 69 (6).

Yanagawa-ke. 1940–1941. *Ōshōmura Chūbu-daiichi Tochi Kukaku Seiri Kumiai Bunsho Tsuzuri* [File of Documents Related to the Ōshōmura Chūbu-daiichi Land Readjustment Association], (Amagasaki Municipal Archives, YANAGAWA Keiichi Papers (2): 826–4).

Yokota, Kusaburō. 1935. *Kumiai setsuritsu made no junbi* [Preparations for the Establishment of an Association]. *Kukaku Seiri* [Land Readjustment] 1 (1).

Chapter 2
Housing Reconstruction in War-Damaged Cities: The Creation and Distribution of Living Spaces in the Late 1940s Under Postwar Governmental Controls

Hiroshi Ono

Abstract This article examines the history of housing reconstruction in postwar Japan, that is, the construction of urban residential housing following Japan's defeat in World War II, providing a historical account of the reconstruction of war-damaged housing from the perspective of the creation and distribution of private residential space under Japan's postwar regulatory regimes. Methodologically, rather than examining the "postwar housing shortage" using the framework of the prewar, peacetime "housing shortage", this article argues that the postwar housing situation was an historically unique situation different from the preceding and subsequent eras. The article systematically examines the process under which Japan's regulatory regime created and distributed non-commercial, residential housing, during a period when various controls blocked the formation of a system based on commercial supply. It assesses this process in terms of the destruction of the supply structure and changes in the ownership structure.

In terms of the creation of non-commercial, residential housing, the article shows how government-controlled materials, capital and residential land were used. Finally the article describes the role of nepotism in the distribution of non-commercial, residential housing, on a rental basis to all levels of society.

Keywords Living spaces • House rent control • Housing shortage • Post-war controls • Rented houses • Room-renting

This chapter is a translation of an article that originally appeared in *Shakai Keizai Shigaku* 79(2) (August 2013), pp. 47–68.

H. Ono (✉)
Faculty of Economics, Kumamoto Gakuen University,
2-5-1, Ōe, Chūō-ku, Kumamoto 862-8680, Japan
e-mail: onohiroshi@kumagaku.ac.jp

S. Baba (ed.), *Economic History of Cities and Housing*, Monograph Series of the Socio-Economic History Society, Japan, DOI 10.1007/978-981-10-4097-9_2

1 Introduction

This aim of this paper is to elucidate the collective experience of the Japanese people in the so-called 'recovery from the ruins'[1] of World War II, through a case study of late-1940s Tokyo and the creation and distribution of 'living spaces,'[2] or 'lived spaces,'[3] which were 'de-commodified' under post-war government controls. The research enumerates the factors that contributed to the reconstruction of living spaces destroyed by the war, and clarifies the relationships among them in the context of 'post-war control'[4] by the government. While critically examining previous

[1] In general, the term 'recovery' carries the strong connotation of 'reconstruction.' Therefore, the image of 'recovery' evoked by the terms 'reconstruction' and 'living space' is that of new housing construction. Indeed, the late 1940s, which is the subject of this study, was a period of construction. During the 5 years between 1945 and 1949, about 2 million houses were built through self-funded construction activities by those in the private sector, even allowing for the small differences that arise depending on which statistical estimation methods are used. Viewed simply in terms of the average number of houses built annually, the construction pace in this period was much higher than in the peacetime pre-war (about 0.3 million houses a year), although the quality of the houses was much poorer. However, this simple basis is not adequate for comparing housing construction under the government's post-war controls with the peacetime housing supply, which responded to effective demand through market mechanisms. Two core elements operated in the construction of urban space during peacetime: the market mechanism and government policy (including urban development policy and housing policy). In the war-damaged cities of the late 1940s, the market mechanism was almost wholly dysfunctional due to government controls, on the one hand, while government interventions in construction remained limited, on the other. Therefore, in order to understand post-war reconstruction from the point of view of 'living spaces,' it is important to investigate empirically the creation and distribution of the various kinds of 'living spaces' that were shaped by government controls.

[2] A few terms used here in relation to 'living spaces' need first to be defined. A 'house' is a building for a household, or households, to inhabit on a constant basis. In the case of the post-war period, a 'house' usually designates the type of dwelling that accommodated a single household. (For instance, a detached house or a unit in a multiple-dwelling complex.) It should be noted in this regard that, in pre-war cities, a house was not necessarily inhabited just by a single household. The term, 'living space,' on the other hand, refers to all forms of space in which people actually dwelt. In this sense, demands for dwelling places were practically met in 'living spaces.' Therefore, 'living spaces' in this study include, apart from the ordinary dwelling places mentioned above: (1) facilities not originally constructed as dwellings (factories, shops, warehouses, schools, remodeled streetcars and so on); (2) non-houses (such as air-raid shelters and provisional huts); and (3) rented rooms, which were living spaces newly created by dividing up a house's original living space. In short, the notion of 'house' emphasizes the physical aspect of the entity in relation to the original purpose of the building. By contrast, 'living space' is a notion that is more related to the act of living and the use of the space for living purposes.

[3] Ryūichi Narita stresses that an important perspective in urban history research is the notion of 'the space in which people lived,' as symbolizing people's lives (Narita 2003). This study uses the term 'living space,' in this vein. Moreover, in consideration of the special historical situation of the period in question, the term 'lived space' is also used to emphasize this 'lived' aspect.

[4] In this study, the term 'post-war control' is used in a broad sense. It indicates any attempt by the government to place controls on the social and economic turmoil of the post-defeat period. Therefore, it includes not only the control on rents, construction and building materials, but also measures such as the Emergency Financial Measures Ordinance and the Act on Temporary

investigations into the war-induced housing shortage, it aims to present a new historical perspective on Japan's post-war reconstruction.

The existing historical research on the reconstruction of war-ravaged cities was conducted from the viewpoint of the history of city planning or of architecture. Their main focus of interest was the ideal and the reality of 'post-war reconstruction projects' principally street improvements and land readjustment (Koshizawa 1991; Tiratsoo et al. 2006; Inoue 2012; Hatsuda 2011). Early postwar scholars, by contrast, addressed the 'war-induced housing shortage' and private sector housing reconstruction that proceeded more or less independently of the public sector's reconstruction projects (Nishiyama 1952, p. 16 and Tokyo Daigaku Shakaikagaku Kenkyūsho, 1952 and 1953). According to Nishiyama, the 'war-induced housing shortage' was characterized by: an extreme disparity between those who had their own houses and those who did not; the further deterioration in the living conditions of those whose living environments were already inadequate; and the emergence of extraordinary ways of dwelling (Nishiyama 1952). In the same study, however, Nishiyama stressed that although the war was obviously responsible for the 'war-induced housing shortage,' it was not the only cause. He argued that ascribing all blame to the war would be as fruitless as arguing that all 100 million Japanese were to blame for that war. In Nishiyama's view, the housing shortage predated the war and was merely aggravated by the mass destruction of the air strikes, which affected the upper-middle as well as the working class. It was not that the war alone created the housing problem, he emphasized, but that it added to the problem's depth and breadth. He concluded by pointing out that the housing problem was the inevitable product of the existing capitalist system (Nishiyama 1952, p. 64).

Whereas Nishiyama in 1952 was addressing existing conditions, namely the 'war-induced housing shortage' still persisting at the time, his later work, *Sumai Kōkongaku* [Today's Housing Conditions], was a historical analysis. In this work, he summarized the gist of the reconstruction-period housing problem as an increase in the proportion of high-density, overcrowded homes and a decrease in spacious ones. He also drew attention to the fact that extremely crowded housing conditions had existed in the pre-war period as well, and that spacious houses remained to some extent in the post-war period. He insisted that the core housing issue was the class disparity in housing quality, and that structural inequities had hardly changed between the two periods. In his view, the severe housing shortage caused by the war was merely the exacerbation of a pre-existing housing quality problem (Nishiyama 1989, p. 301).

In Nishiyama's view, in other words, the housing problem derived from the capitalist economic structure, in which the quality of urban housing deteriorated inevitably due to the economic motives of those involved in the housing supply, including financiers, lessors, builders and landowners (Nishiyama 1942, pp. 139–140). The present study does not counter Nishiyama's arguments inasmuch as they pertain to

---

Measures Concerning Land and House Lease in War-damaged Cities. This study thus uses the term 'post-war control' to indicate the whole set of institutional measures that shaped the creation and distribution of living spaces.

the peacetime housing issues of the pre-war period. The capitalist economic structure and economic motives of housing suppliers do not sufficiently account, however, for the war-induced housing shortage, which derived from the wartime air strikes and was shaped by the government's social and economic controls. The early post-war problem was specific to its historical moment, and different in its nature from the type of housing shortage caused by the economic structure of capitalism. It is untenable to argue that the war-induced housing shortage was merely the further deterioration of the pre-war problem and that they differed only in depth and breadth.

This study examines the formation of de-commodified living (or 'lived') spaces in war-stricken cities as a specific historical process, determined, in the main, by post-war government controls. It aims thereby to serve as a complement to conventional historical research on the post-war reconstruction and creation of urban space, which has addressed only the public aspect of the recovery, namely the planning and implementation of government's reconstruction projects. By contrast, this study draws attention to the decision-making of economic agents involved in the formation of private living spaces and how these decisions were shaped by the government's control policies. In short, it seeks to shed new light on post-war reconstruction through a focus on how living spaces were created and distributed under a system of government controls.

2 Structural Changes in Living Spaces

2.1 A Statistical Look at Supply and Demand in Housing

Two significant changes occurred after the interwar period with regard to housing stock in war-stricken cities. The first was the absolute decrease in the housing stock due to air strikes and building removals.[5] The second was the rapid fall in the proportion of rented houses to the total number of houses. During the interwar period, houses leased by small- and medium-sized homeowners constituted a large part of the housing supply, with the proportions of rented houses hovering around 80% in major cities.[6] The rental rate dropped throughout the 1940s, however, especially in war-stricken cities. In Tokyo's case, rented houses accounted for only 34.9% of the total in 1950, almost a 40-percentage point decline from the pre-war period (Sōri-fu Tōkei-kyoku 1954a, p. 263). The decrease in the proportion of rented houses, however, did not necessarily entail an increase in the proportion of owned houses. In fact, only 46.4% of total households dwelt in their own houses, a figure that seems

[5] Japan's housing stock immediately after the end of the war is estimated to have been short by 4.2 million homes. Most of these losses were concentrated in war-damaged cities (Jūtaku Kin'yū Kōko 1960, p. 3).

[6] As of November 1941, rented houses accounted for 78.4% of total houses; owned houses, 20.1%; and issued houses, 1.5% (Kōsei-shō Jūtaku-kyoku 1942, p. 14).

incompatible with the huge decline in the proportion of rented houses. In the late 1940s, in particular, the contradiction between the low rate of house rentals and the low rate of house-ownership is particularly conspicuous. To account for the seeming incompatibility, we must consider how much 'room-renting' was taking place, and also conduct empirical investigations into the actual state of owned houses. Many such owned houses were built on leased lands immediately after the end of the war, through self-funded construction by those in the private sector.

2.1.1 The Supply-Demand Balance in Housing

Before proceeding with the discussion, let us examine the statistical data on housing supply and demand. Table 2.1 shows changes in the number of houses completed each year in the Tokyo metropolitan area. From August through December of 1945, around 10,000 houses were completed, with an average area of 9.9 *tsubo* (approximately 32.7 m^2). This figure includes many provisional dwelling facilities. In September 1945, 227,000 people in Tokyo (9.4% of Tokyo's total population) were still living in underground shelters and provisional huts (Tokyo-to 1953, p. 519). Between 1946 and 1947, the number of completed houses continued to rise, surpassing 40,000. Their average area also increased to above 14 *tsubo* (approximately 46.3 m^2). 1948, however, saw a decline in the number of houses completed, and their average area shrank to the 12-*tsubo* (39.7 m^2) level. Although the number of completed houses rose again in 1949, their average area did not rise.

These changes in the number of completed houses and their average area occurred under the specific socio-economic circumstances of post-war Japan, in particular the strong governmental controls on construction and the distribution of building materials. This study will examine empirically what kinds of economic agencies in the private sector contributed to the reconstruction of 'owned houses' and in what way.

Turning to the supply-demand balance in housing in this period, Table 2.1 shows that about 800,000 houses were demolished during the war by air strikes and building removals, while the number of households increased by as many as 720,000 immediately after the war. The number of houses built by the end of 1945 accounted for only 1.4% of the increase in the number of households. This generated an enormous supply-demand gap. Despite repeated administrative attempts to restrict incomers and to encourage people to move out of the Tokyo metropolitan area, the number of households in the area kept rising at far higher rates than the number of newly completed houses. As a result, the vacancy rate (the ratio of the number of vacant houses to the total number of houses) remained as low as 0.1–0.3%. The dire housing shortage persisted throughout the late 1940s. The enormous supply-demand gap notwithstanding, however, people still required spaces in which to live. The wider the supply-demand gap, therefore, the more necessary the sharing and redistribution of existing living spaces became, simply because the gap had to be filled. As Nishiyama has pointed out, therefore, attention should be paid to 'house-sharing' as a means of coping with the housing shortage. The 'high-density housing'

Table 2.1 Population and numbers of households, vacant houses and completed houses in Tokyo

Year	Population (thousand persons)[a]		Number of households (a) (thousand households)		Number of household members (persons)	Number of vacant houses[a] (b) (thousand houses)	Vacancy rate (b/a)	Completed houses[b]			Increase in number of houses (e) (thousand households)	Number of houses lost[a] (f) (thousand houses)	Supply-demand gap (b + c − e − f)
	Actual number	Index	Actual number	Index				Number (c) (thousand houses)	Area (d) (thousand *tsubo*: 3306 m²)	d/c			
1945 (August–December)	2883	100	724	100	3.98	1	0.1%	10	102	9.9	724	803	−1515
1946	3620	126	895	124	4.05	1	0.1%	46	646	14.2	171	1	−125
1947	4178	145	1003	139	4.17	1	0.1%	48	705	14.6	108	1	−62
1948	4511	156	1077	149	4.19	3	0.2%	35	437	12.5	74	1	−35
1949	4947	172	1187	164	4.17	4	0.3%	64	823	12.8	110	2	−43

Sources:
[a]Keishichō [The Tokyo Metropolitan Police Department], Keishichō Tōkeisho [The Tokyo Metropolitan Police Department Statistics Book]
[b]Kensetsu-shō Jūtaku-kyoku [The Ministry of Construction, Housing Bureau], Jūtakunenkan 1951 [Housing Yearbook 1951]: pp. 266–277 and 280–281

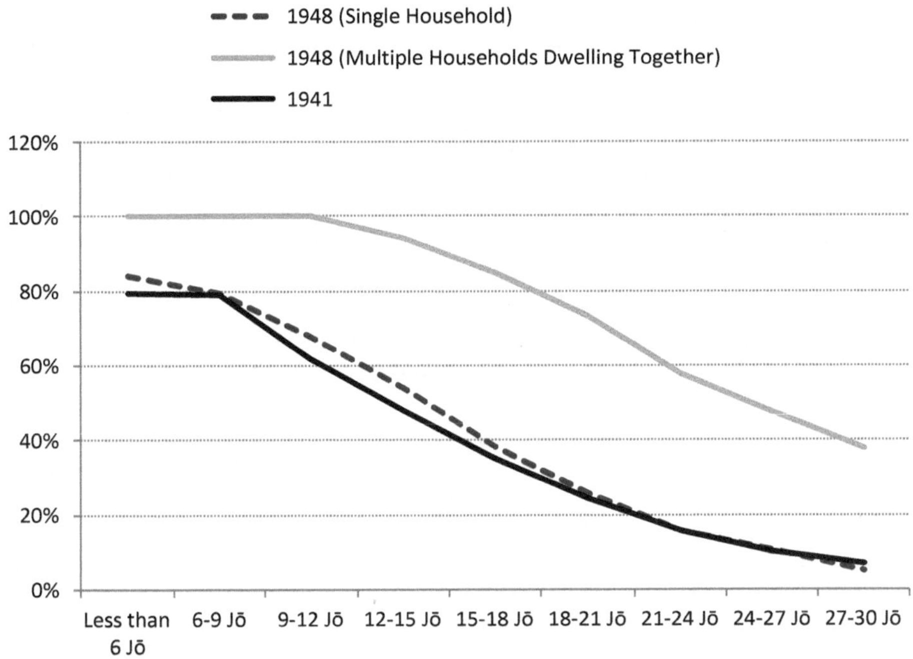

Fig. 2.1 Proportions of high-density houses by floor area, Tokyo (*Sources*: Kōsei-shō Seikatsu-kyoku [The Ministry of Welfare, Living Bureau], *Shōwa 16 Nen Daitoshi Jūtakuchōsa Tōkeihyō* [Statistics Tables of the 1941 Large Cities Housing Survey] (1942): p. 60. Kensetsu-shō Kenchiku-kyoku Jūtakukikaku-ka [The Ministry of Construction, Construction Bureau, Housing Planning Section] *Shōwa 23 Nen Jūtakuchōsa Shuyōtoshi Kyojū Jin'inbetsu Kyojūshitsu Jōsūbetsu Kosūgaisū* [The 1948 Housing Survey, Approximate Numbers of Houses in Large Cities by Number of Residents and by Floor Area] (1949): p. 73. Note: A 'high-density house' is defined as a house of which the average dwelling area per person was less than 3 jō (1 jō = 1.82 m^2). The numbers only concern houses used exclusively for residential purposes. Dwelling houses used for other (commercial) purposes are not included)

phenomenon that resulted from house-sharing was one of the fundamental characteristics of the war-induced housing shortage (Nishiyama 1989, p. 297).

Figure 2.1 shows the difference in the proportions of high-density houses by floor area in 1941 and 1948. For 1948, houses are divided into two categories: those lived in only by single households and those in which multiple households dwelled together – that is, houses with rooms rented to other households. The proportional distribution pattern of 1941 is almost identical to the single households' pattern of 1948, even though the proportions of 1948 are slightly higher in general. This supports Nishiyama's view that the disparity among social classes remained unchanged. However, the line representing the ratio of high-density houses to multiple-household houses in 1948 is well above that of 1941. While Nishiyama stresses the unchanged structural disparity among social classes, the figures presented here show that, regardless of differences in house size, room-renting was a widespread practice in all social classes. The government's policy, based on the 1946 amendment of the 1945 Emergency Housing Measures Ordinance, of utilizing 'houses with sufficient space' for families that had lost their houses, proved a failure, since only 400 out of 3400 'houses with sufficient space' in Tokyo (11.8%) were used in this way. At the same time, in 'houses without sufficient space,' which accounted for more than 99% of all houses that had survived the war, a large number of rooms had already been rented privately even before the amendment of the Emergency Housing Measures Ordinance. This points to an important aspect of private-sector reconstruction efforts that previous studies, focused mainly on public reconstruction projects, have failed to grasp. The government's official housing-supply policy had to be supplemented by self-funded reconstruction efforts by those who had been bombed out of their homes. The practice of room-renting (redistribution of living spaces) that spread in all social classes played a crucial role in providing places for people to live.

As of September 1945, 687,000 people in Tokyo (28.5% of Tokyo's population) were living at their relatives' places (Tokyo-to 1953, p. 519). While air-raid shelters and provisional huts gradually ceased to play their temporary roles during and after 1946, room-renting remained an important practice and numerically significant throughout the late 1940s. Room-renting, which spread among all social classes, naturally raised density levels, while lowering the average number of people constituting a household, from 4.72 in Tokyo in 1940, to 3.90 in 1946 (Tokyo-to Sōmu-kyoku Tōkei-bu 1955, p. 34). This number, though rising again to 4.29 in 1950, remained below its pre-war level, and many cases still obtained of family members' living separately (Nishiyama 1952, pp. 1–7). This fragmentation of living spaces curbed the increase in the number of people constituting a household. The creation of new living spaces through self-funded construction activities by those in the private sector faced various obstacles.

2.1.2 Regional Disparities

During the interwar period, the housing market in Tokyo grew concentrically, in accordance with the development of the modern transport system. At the same time, however, the market also reflected regional characteristics that derived from a given area's historical background, as for instance in the case of the 'Yamanote (uptown)' and 'Shitamachi (downtown)' districts. An enormous number of houses in the central and eastern part of Tokyo were burned down in wartime air raids, which further complicated housing disparities by creating gaps between war-damaged and unaffected areas, and between those bombed out of their homes and those whose homes remained intact. The following section examines regional disparities in housing reconstruction with reference to Table 2.2. Note that Table 2.2 divides Tokyo into four areas.

Area I corresponds to the eastern part of Tokyo, comprising residential and industrial districts. This was a high population density area, where the proportion of damaged houses was 84%, the highest among the four areas. As of 1951, this area had recovered only 46% of its 1941 housing level, the lowest among the areas.

Table 2.2 Tokyo's population and number of houses by area (index numbers: 1941 = 100)

	1945		1951	
	Population	Number of houses	Population	Number of houses
I	13	16	53	46
II	28	31	69	68
III	51	61	101	89
IV	76	91	135	114
Total	35	42	80	73

Sources: Tokyo-to Kenchiku-kyoku Sōmu-bu. Kikaku-ka [The Tokyo Metropolitan Government, Construction Bureau, General Affairs Department, Planning Section], Tokyo-to Jūtakunenpō 1956 [The Tokyo Annual Housing Report 1956] (1957): pp. 36–37. Keishichō [The Tokyo Metropolitan Police Department], Keishichō Tōkeisho [The Tokyo Metropolitan Police Department Statistics Book]

Notes: Area I. The 1951 housing recovery rates were less than 60%. Kōtō, Sumida, Arakawa and Taitō Wards

Area II. The 1951 housing recovery rates were less than 75%. Chūō, Bunkyō, Minato, Chiyoda, Ōta, Shinagawa, Shinjuku, Shibuya and Toshima Wards

Area III. The 1951 housing recovery rates were less than 100%. Kita, Meguro, Edogawa, Suginami and Nakano Wards

Area IV. The 1951 housing recovery rates were more than 100%. Itabashi, Nerima, Katsushika, Setagaya and Adachi Wards. The 1951 Housing Recovery Rate (%) = Number of Houses of 1951/ Number of Houses of 1941 × 100

This area had the highest growth rates in both population and number of houses among the four areas during these years, but the absolute levels of the indexes of population and number of houses were far below the pre-war levels, because of the magnitude of the destruction caused by air raids. In Area I, reconstruction was still only halfway along as of 1951. Area II consists of three wards in the center of Tokyo and the residential areas along the Yamanote railway line. This area included many high population density districts, and the proportion of damaged houses was 70%, the second highest after Area I. Housing had recovered to 68% of its pre-war levels in 1951. It is notable that in Area II, in 1951, the population index and the index of the number of houses are almost the same. Area III, located outside the war-stricken areas, had damage and recovery rates of 39 and 89%, respectively. That is, its damage rate was moderate and its recovery rate relatively high, and its population index in 1951 exceeds the index of the number of houses the same year. Area IV consists of suburbs with low population density, where the damage rate was only 9%. With more than 90% of houses having survived the war, its housing recovery rate was 114%, the highest among the four areas. Although the number of houses in 1951 is at the pre-war level, the index of population far exceeds the index of the number of houses. There is a considerable gap between them.

On the basis of these findings, regional characteristics as they related to the degree of war damage can be summarized as follows: In areas where damage rates were high, population inflow was checked by the shortage of houses. In fact, the populations of such areas remained under 1941 levels even in 1951. In addition, the indexes for both population and number of houses rose at almost the same pace, with only a very small gap between them. This indicates that self-help construction efforts by those who suffered war damage made a crucial contribution to the rise in the number of houses. By contrast, in areas where damage rates were relatively low, the number of houses had almost reached, or already exceeded, pre-war levels by 1951. Population inflow, however, was proceeding at a higher pace than the growth in the number of houses. The population index increased more rapidly than the index of the number of houses. This indicates that while new living spaces were being created, existing living spaces in houses that had survived the war were being redistributed fairly actively.

2.2 *The 'De-commodification' of Living Spaces*

2.2.1 The Destruction of the Housing Supply Structure Through House-Rent Controls

One of the crucial factors affecting the housing supply during the 1940s was the house-rent control implemented by the government both during and after the war. After the outbreak of the Second Sino-Japanese War in 1937, the government gradually expanded the areas over which it exerted control and imposed price controls on a wide range of goods and services as part of its war-economy controls. House rents, which constituted an important part of household expenditure, were put under government control in October 1939, with the promulgation of the First Land and House Rent Control Ordinance. Controls on house rents were maintained until July 1950, when rent control on newly built leased houses was removed. (House-rent controls were not completely removed until 1986.) Meanwhile, the Second Land and House Rent Control Ordinance, issued in October 1940, guaranteed a certain minimum profit rate for new investments in rental houses. However, the 1941 amendment of the House Lease Act and the growing shortage of building materials made investments in rental houses less and less attractive, and the supply of houses for rent shrank as a result.

Controls on house rent regulated the supply of rental houses not only during, but after the war as well. According to a questionnaire survey of rental-house associations and governors, it was widely held that rent control should be maintained after the end of the war because an abrupt rise in house rents could threaten the stability of people's living circumstances. Nevertheless, given the explosive inflation of the early post-war years, the government's rent control policy faced serious contradictions: illegally high rents were spreading, killing the effects of government controls, while at the same time, the official controls on rent were making it difficult for the government to encourage the construction and repair of rental houses.

The GHQ urged the Japanese government to take immediate action to maintain effective control over house rents. The Third Land and House Rent Control Ordinance was therefore put into effect in October 1946, and official house rent levels were raised. The increased rents were calculated by multiplying 'frozen house-rent prices' (rents effective 30 September, 1946) by certain rates set according to the age of the property. Land rates, meanwhile, remained fixed at the 'frozen land-rent prices.' The Ordinance allowed house owners to raise rents above the official level so that they could pay for repair expenses. The amount of the raise had to be limited to a range that was affordable for the tenants, but in any event, the main purpose of such provisions in the Ordinance was to encourage owners to repair the rented houses. Rent increases by house owners had to be approved by local governors. In this sense, rents were subject to control and approval, calculated as the sum of the land rent and the building cost, multiplied by a certain fixed rate. The obligation of notification was imposed on all owners of rental land and houses, and all rents were therefore made public at local government offices.

After the Third Land and House Rent Control Ordinance, official rents were gradually raised as inflation accelerated. Table 2.3 compares the changes in the actual rent of a leased house located in Tsukishima, Chūō Ward, Tokyo, with the changes in Tokyo's official, controlled rents. It is evident that actual rents rose relatively quickly following revisions in the official price. During the pre-war period, house rents generally followed consumer price trends with a time lag of a few years, notwithstanding the downward price rigidity of house rents. Under post-war controls, house owners were required only to notify their tenants of upcoming rent revisions, but rents at the time were worth only something like two packs of cigarettes.

Because the increase in the official, controlled house rents could not keep pace with the explosive rise in consumer prices, house rents dropped considerably in real terms. The Pricing Agency recognized the need to raise official rents in the face of accelerating inflation, but could not agree to the removal of the rent controls for fear of destabilizing people's housing situations. It should be noted here that the Third Land and House Rent Control Ordinance issued after the war differed significantly in intent from the wartime Second Land and House Rent Control Ordinance. The Second Ordinance aimed, among other things, to stimulate the housing supply by guaranteeing a minimum profit on investments in the construction of rental houses. The purpose of the Third Ordinance, however, was to maintain the extent of existing rental houses in the face of steep plunge in real rents. The class of people who profited most from the Third Ordinance were those tenants who continued to dwell, from the pre-war period, in the same rented houses that had survived the war, paying only the minimum required official rent. Those who had been bombed out of their homes, on the other hand – that is, those whose living situation was most unstable – could not enjoy these benefits.

The post-war control of house rents, as one of the countermeasures against inflation, led to the overutilization of those rental houses that had narrowly escaped air raids during the war and also to the complete destruction of the operating basis of the house-renting business. According to Table 2.4, which shows the official and actual rents per *tsubo* (approximately 3.3 m^2) and the cost of managing rental houses, actual rents were about 10 yen higher than official rents and about 40 yen lower than the break-even price for the lender. Furthermore, the actual rent level was slightly below the price payable by tenants. This indicates that tenants' capacity to

Table 2.3 Actual rent of existing house, official house rent, wooden building construction cost index and wholesale price index (1940, March = 100)

Actual rent price of house owned by Mr. O			Official house rent price ('frozen rent price')					
Time of revision	Monthly payment (yen)	Index number	Time of revision	Average price per Tsubo (3.3 m²)	Index number	Year/month	Wooden house construction cost index (Tokyo)	Wholesale price index (Tokyo)
1935 June	28	100	1939 November	—	—		...	...
	28	100		—	—	1939 March	73	85
	28	100		1.48	100		...	...
	28	100		1.48	100	1940 March	100	100
1946 March	28	100	1946 October	1.50	101	1946 March	1490	726
	28	100		1.48	100		...	...
1946 November	60	214	1947 September	1.48	100		...	...
	60	214		1.48	100	1947 March	3462	1472
	60	214		3.70	250	1947 September	4815	4043
1948 March	67	239		3.70	250	1948 March	6560	5264
	67	239		3.70	250	1948 September	8706	10,347
1948 October	168	598	1948 October	9.25	625		...	...
	168	598		9.25	625	1949 March	10,447	11,964
1949 June	268	957	1949 June	14.85	1003		...	...
	268	957		14.85	1003	1949 September	9915	13,172
	268	957		14.85	1003	1950 March	8775	13,802
1950 August	900	3214	1950 August	40.38	2728		...	...
	900	3214		40.38	2728	1950 September	10,108	15,838

Source: *Kashiya Chinryō Ryōshūshō* (privately owned documents). Tokyo-to Kenchiku-kyoku Sōmu-bu. Kikaku-ka [The Tokyo Metropolitan Government, Construction Bureau, General Affairs Department, Planning Section], *Tokyo-to Jūtakunenpō* 1957 [The Tokyo Annual Housing Report 1957] (1958): p. 80. Nihon Kangyō Ginkō Chōsa-bu. [The Nihon Kangyō Bank, Research Department], Zenkoku Mokuzō Kenchikuhi Shisū ni tsuite [On the Wooden Building Construction Cost Index] (1954): p. 8

Table 2.4 House rent and management cost of rented house per *tsubo* (3.3 m^2)

	House rent		Management cost of rented house						
Floor area (tsubo)	Official house rent (yen/tsubo)(a)	Actual house rent (yen/tsubo)(b)	Actual Land Rent (yen/tsubo)	Repair expenses, property tax, etc. (yen/tsubo)	Total (c)	b – c	Break-even rent price for the house owner (d) (yen/tsubo)	b – d	Rent price payable by tenants (yen/tsubo)
15.1	43.3	53.5	9.0	67.3	76.3	–22.8	93.5	–40.0	56.7

Source: Nihon Kenchiku Gakkai Kenchiku Keizai Iinkai [The Architectural Institute of Japan, the Construction and Economy Committee], *Kenchiku Keizai Tōkeisiryō* [Statistical Data on Construction and Economy] (1952): pp. 38–39

Note: The research objects are rented houses that had been rented continuously in the Tokyo Metropolitan Area from 30 September, 1946 through November, 1950 pay was the crucial factor in determining actual rents. The swelling of food expenses, in particular, made housing a relatively small proportion of household expenditures. In Tokyo, food expenses rose from 33.7 to 61.6% of total consumer spending between 1935–1936 and 1946–1947, while housing expenses dropped from 18.4 to 3.6% during the same period (Tokyo-to Sōmu-bu Tōkei-ka 1947, pp. 4–10). Land and house rents only accounted for 0.89% of total housing expenses (Honjō 1948, p. 36). Illegally high rents were often demanded when house leasehold contracts were made with new tenants, but only rarely imposed in renewals of existing contracts (Kensetsu-shō Jūtaku-kyoku 1951, p. 107). In this sense, rent controls can be understood to have functioned relatively effectively so far as long-term tenants were concerned. Pre-war tenants who had hardly been affected by the air raids now enjoyed the benefit of a considerable decline in real rents, due to the government's rent controls. They were thus able to regain their footing at the expense of the house owners' gains. The accelerating inflation meanwhile pushed up the cost to house owners of renting out houses. According to Table 2.4, the per-*tsubo* (3.3 m^2) cost of renting out houses surpassed actual house rents by about 23 yen. House owners thus incurred losses merely by maintaining their rental houses. Since rent prices were set officially, house owners had no choice but to reduce costs in order to earn a profit. They were practically forced to cut repair expenses, in particular, as reducible costs, since land rents and taxes were irreducible fixed costs. Even the minimum necessary repair work was not undertaken on many rental houses. In 1953, about 30% of houses in the Tokyo metropolitan area were considered in need of repair due to damage and rot (Sōri-fu Tōkei-kyoku 1954b, pp. 114–115). Regulations on prices of goods and services were gradually abolished as the Dodge Line – the financial and monetary contraction policy designed by Joseph Morrell Dodge – began to bring inflation under control, and controls on the rent of newly constructed houses were lifted in July 1950. Rent control continued to apply to old houses, however.

2.2.2 Changes in the Ownership Structure: From Rented House to Owned House

One of the reasons for the increase in the proportion of owned houses during the 1940s was the gradual shift in the ownership of rented houses during this period from former owners to tenants. This change was precipitated by the government's rent control policy and the rise in maintenance costs. After the outbreak of the Second Sino-Japanese War, an increasing number of house owners sought to sell off their rental houses because of the low prospects for making a profit. Many disputes arose between house owners and tenants over such issues as owners' refusal to renew existing leasehold contracts. In 1941, the Land and House Price Control Ordinance was issued to prevent speculative trading in housing. At the same time, the House Lease Law was amended, such that house owners could not reject the renewal of existing contracts without justification. While the profitability of the house-renting business declined, tenants' rights became considerably stronger.

At the same time, the controls on real estate prices were not removed. House owners therefore tended to sell their rental houses when their tenants moved out.

As has been elucidated above, the shift from rented to owned houses was already underway during the war. After the end of the war, the explosive inflation and the maintenance of rent control accelerated this process, driving the house-renting business into the red. Furthermore, in November 1946, a property tax was introduced with the aim of securing government revenue and correcting the disparity in the distribution of wealth (Arai and Nagai 1946). A progressive taxation system was applied on properties worth more than 100,000 yen. In fiscal 1948, moreover, houses that had not been damaged by the war became subject to taxation, while land and house taxes were raised seven and five times, respectively (Tani 1950). The tax pressure spurred house owners to release their rental houses, on the one hand, while those who purchased these properties began to constitute a new house-owners' class, on the other. A 'victim' of the price restriction policy, real property became a mere means of taxation (Tokyodaigaku Shakaikagaku Kenkyūsho 1953, p. 263). According to a 1952 inquiry into why house owners lost their rental houses, the top reason (67.2%) was 'destruction by air raid or building removal.' However, in the case of rental houses that had survived the war, the top reason (63.2%) was 'sold to tenants' and the second reason (17.1%) was 'payment in kind' (Kensetsu-shō 1953).

The next question to be asked is what class of people purchased the properties disposed of under such circumstances. According to a survey conducted in three areas in Tokyo, 33.5% of houses built during the pre-war period were sold after the war (Tokyodaigaku Shakaikagaku Kenkyūsho 1952, p. 88). This means that about a third of the houses that had survived the war changed owners in the 3 or 4 years after the end of the war. The occupations of the purchasers included a high proportion of self-employed businessmen, liberal professions (such as doctors and lawyers) and corporate executives. In many cases, upper-income people, or those who had accumulated funds under the special economic circumstance of the post-war period, purchased the rental houses released in this way to use them for their own residences.

In July 1950, rent controls were lifted on newly built rental houses. However, rents for existing rental houses were maintained at a low level. The operating basis of the house-renting business was completely shattered during the wartime-to-post-war period of government controls. The introduction of the property tax and the increase in the real estate tax drove traditional house owners to dispose of their rental houses. A case study of Shitaya Ward (present-day Taitō Ward) found that, as of March 1949, not one house owner was operating a house-renting business on the same scale as in the pre-war period (Tokyodaigaku Shakaikagaku Kenkyūsho 1952, p. 203). Even those house owners who had escaped war damage had in many cases reduced the scale of their house-renting businesses by 1949, by releasing their rental houses. According to a 1952 questionnaire survey on the management of the house-renting business, the number of house owners who wanted to sell their rental houses (36.8%) was far greater than the number of house owners who wanted to build new rental houses (2.5%) (Kensetsu-shō Jūtaku-kyoku 1953, pp. 179–181). Among traditional house owners who had rented out houses from the pre-war into the post-war years, interest in new investments in rental houses had largely diminished. Even after rent control was lifted, it took some time before interest in the business was restored.

3 The Private Sector's Self-Funded Construction Activities Under Post-war Controls

Towards the end of the war, the housing shortage problem for those who had been bombed out of their homes remained untouched, without any proposals for concrete countermeasures (The Asahi Newspaper, 13 January, 1945). The housing construction that was carried out immediately after the end of the war has been assessed rather negatively for the general public's lack of understanding of city planning, the failure to realize the plans, and the over-construction of illegal buildings (Tiratsoo et al. 2006, pp. 298–301). However, the actual state of housing construction activities has not yet been fully investigated. This section will examine the conditions under which living spaces were created in war-damaged cities through the private sector's self-funded reconstruction efforts. The examination is organized around three basic elements: materials, funds and lands.

3.1 Constraints on Building Materials

3.1.1 Regional Disparities in the Availability of Wood Materials and Their Procurement Methods

The first element to consider is wood materials, because they were indispensable to the construction of Japanese houses and because their availability shaped the reconstruction activities of the private sector. This section is a comprehensive examination of the methods used to procure building materials under the post-war government's controls, along with the relationship between changes in the supply-demand balance with respect to materials and the controls on materials and construction.

When the war ended, the government at first adopted deregulation policies regarding controls on construction and building materials. In November 1945, Regulations on the Rationing of Wood Materials were amended, so that distributors of wood materials became able to run their business without a license and collect and distribute wood materials freely within their prefectures (The Asahi Newspaper, 27 November 1945). In addition, Regulations on Building were abolished in December of the same year. As a consequence of these measures, illegal construction thrived in war-damaged cities: Housing reconstruction stagnated, but buildings for commercial use (for amusement, in particular) were constructed rapidly (Kenchiku-kyoku Kantoku-ka, 1946, p. 9). The reconstruction of amusement districts was largely dependent on illegal construction. In any event, the reconstruction of housing for the general public was a completely different matter (Watari 1948, p. 122).

Wood production had plummeted from 100 million *koku* (approximately 27.8 million cubic meters) to 65 million *koku* (18.1 million cubic meters) from 1944 through 1945. This, together with the inefficient transportation system, caused regional disparities in the availability of wood materials (Shinrinshigen Sōgōtaisaku Kyōgikai 1951, p. 6). In places such as Tokyo where the demand for building materials was great, the shortage of such basic materials as wood was the greatest obstacle to housing reconstruction (Tokyo Shiseichōsakai Tokyo-to Sōmu-bu Chōsa-ka 1947, pp. 2–3). In contrast to the rather rapid recovery of housing construction in wood-producing provincial areas, housing reconstruction in wood-consuming prefectures, including the five major cities, lagged far behind (Kenchiku-kyoku Jūtaku-ka 1946a, p. 24). As of 31 March 1946, Tokyo's reconstruction rate (the proportion of completed houses to the estimated number of houses destroyed by the war) was as low as 6.1%, as against the national average of 9.5%. The gap reflected the regional disparity in the availability of wood materials. Local governments were unwilling to export wood to other prefectures, preferring to supply the scarce resource to local areas in their own prefectures. Those in need of wood materials, meanwhile, attempted to negotiate directly with mountain owners, bypassing the official routes regulated by the government. As a result, illegal construction spread in defiance of the War Damage Reconstruction Agency's official plans, while the wood that was produced was retained in provincial areas (The Asahi Newspaper, 15 December 1946).

Because of the uneven distribution of wood materials and the emergence of black markets, the amount of wood materials supplied through official routes was much smaller than the amount allotted in the rationing plan. Although Tokyo was allotted 228.9 thousand *koku* (approximately 637 thousand cubic meters) of wood in fiscal 1946, the actual amount supplied through the rationing system was only 838 thousand *koku* (approximately 233 thousand cubic meters: 37%). Meanwhile, however, 349.1 thousand *koku* of wood materials (approximately 972 thousand cubic meters, 4.2 times the amount supplied through the official rationing system) was imported to Tokyo through unofficial means (Tokyo Shiseichōsakai Tokyo-to Sōmu-bu Chōsa-ka 1947, p. 18). In other words, three quarters of the total wood materials imported into Tokyo came through unofficial routes.

Let us turn to an examination of the concrete measures taken to import into Tokyo the wood materials used for the construction of new houses. According to an inquiry conducted in April 1946, the largest proportion of imported wood (30%) was obtained through 'black markets'; the second most important source (24%) was 'evacuated or war-damaged materials'; the third most important source (21%) was 'agents (of black markets).' (Tokyo-to Kenchiku-ka 1946, pp. 7–8) 'Evacuated or war-damaged materials' had been used for the construction of emergency housing facilities such as air-raid shelters and provisional huts from the closing stages of the war through the war's immediate aftermath. By the end of 1946, however, they were no longer in use for this purpose. Still, only 15% of the materials were obtained at official prices through the rationing system. Although those with assets were able to acquire materials through ‘agents,’ others had to pursue every possible avenue. According to an inquiry conducted by the War Damage Reconstruction Agency, the most common means of obtaining materials was ‘through relatives and friends,’ followed by ‘through black market agents.’ The latter measure was adopted by those who possessed a large amount of ‘new yen’ (Usui et al. 1947, p. 5).

As has been shown, from the closing stages of the war through 1946, materials for the construction of new houses in war-stricken cities were procured through routes other than the official one set by the government. Under the social and economic circumstances that obtained immediately after the end of the war, it was difficult to procure building materials without special personal connections or funds sufficient for black-market prices. As of January 1947, the actual price of wood was 5.8 times the official price (Tokyo Shiseichōsakai Tokyo-to Sōmu-bu Chōsa-ka 1947, p. 19). Black markets expanded because of the difficulty of controlling the prices and circulation of building materials such as wood.

3.1.2 The Tightening Supply-Demand Balance for Wood and Controls on Construction and Building Materials

In fiscal 1946, the supply-demand balance with respect to building materials became extremely tight because of the Occupation Forces’ enormous demand for housing. Since the construction of 20 thousand houses for the Occupation Forces was ordered on the basis of ‘On the Matter of the Housing Construction Plan for the Occupation Forces and their Families’ (SCAPIN, No. 799 dated 6 March, 1946), the Japanese government was forced to fundamentally revise its 1946 supply-demand plan for building materials. Around 8 million *koku* (2.2 million cubic meters) of wood was needed for the construction demanded by the Occupation Forces (Koizumi et al. 1999, p. 46). This corresponded to 67% of Japan’s total supply of construction wood estimated for fiscal 1946 (12 million *koku*, 3.3 million cubic meters). Caught between the Occupation Forces’ housing demand and the needs of war-damaged cities, the Japanese government adopted a policy of supplying building materials preferentially for housing construction for workers engaged in ‘strategic industries.’ The supply of materials for war-damaged cities was a lower priority, to be implemented ‘as much as possible.’ Eventually, the government succeeded in providing the building materials demanded by the Occupation Forces. Apart from that, however, the actual amounts of material supplied through the rationing system were far below planned levels. The government’s initial supply-demand plan for building materials was fundamentally revised and housing reconstruction in war-damaged cities became extremely difficult (Shōkō-shō 1946). In order to meet the Occupation Forces’ large housing demand, the Japanese government was forced to restrict the construction of new buildings in war-damaged cities and to reinforce its control over construction and the distribution of building materials.

The Temporary Ordinance on Restrictions on Construction was put to effect in May 1946. It once again tightened the construction regulations that had been loosened immediately after the end of the war. The purpose of the construction controls was to restrict non-urgent construction and to use the materials saved thereby for the reconstruction of houses and schools. Therefore, the Ordinance prohibited the construction of new buildings and the extension and reconstruction of existing ones unless it was urgent. In addition, the area of newly built houses was limited to no more than 15 *tsubo* (approximately 49.5 m^2) (Isahaya 1946, p. 4). The February 1947 Temporary Regulations on the Restriction of Construction then lowered the maximum area permitted for new houses to 12 *tsubo* (approximately 39.6 m^2) – or, for multiuse houses, 15 *tsubo*. The Regulations also required that the construction of new houses and the extension and reconstruction of existing houses not be commenced without permission from the War Damage Reconstruction Agency. The effects of the Regulations are reflected in the average area of completed houses shown in Table 2.1. Although wood's supply-demand balance began to slacken in 1948 because of the decline in the number of new houses constructed, the average area of a new house remained around 12 *tsubo*, the upper limit imposed by the regulations.

When the war ended, the short-term supply-demand balance in building materials slackened because of the release of military materials. In the medium term, however, the balance was not redressed. As the supply-demand balance tightened rapidly in 1946, it once again became imperative for the government to maintain control over the distribution of materials. In October 1946, the Temporary Act on Materials Supply and Demand Adjustment replaced the National Mobilization Law, which had been the legal foundation of the government's control policies (Nōrinsuisan Shizaijuyōshadantai Kyōgikai 1947). Based on this Act, the Economic Stabilization Agency made supply-demand plans for important goods and issued the orders necessary to fulfill these plans. Regulations on the Allotment of Specified Production Materials followed in January 1947. The result was a ration-ticket system through which important materials were strategically allocated (Sensaifukkoin Kenchiku-kyoku Kantoku-ka 1947). With the establishment of Regulations on the Allotment of Specified Production Materials and Temporary Regulations on the Restriction of Construction, the task of allotting building materials and that of issuing construction permits were now both placed under the jurisdiction of the same agency, the War Damage Reconstruction Agency. This meant that the War Damage Reconstruction Agency's rulings on construction permits were now dependent on the amount of materials allocable to the construction plan. In other words, once a building permit had been issued, it was institutionally guaranteed that the materials necessary for the construction would be available at official prices. Without a permit, however, the construction of a new house or the extension or reconstruction of an existing house was utterly impossible.[7] If a person who had lost his house sought to build a house, he could not acquire so much as a piece of board without the luck of drawing a winning ticket at a public office. The government's control on

[7] In fact, the ration tickets did not circulate smoothly from those demanding them through those distributing them to those issuing them. According to estimates by the Economic Stability Agency, only 70% of ration tickets returned to the issuer (Saitō 1948, p. 182).

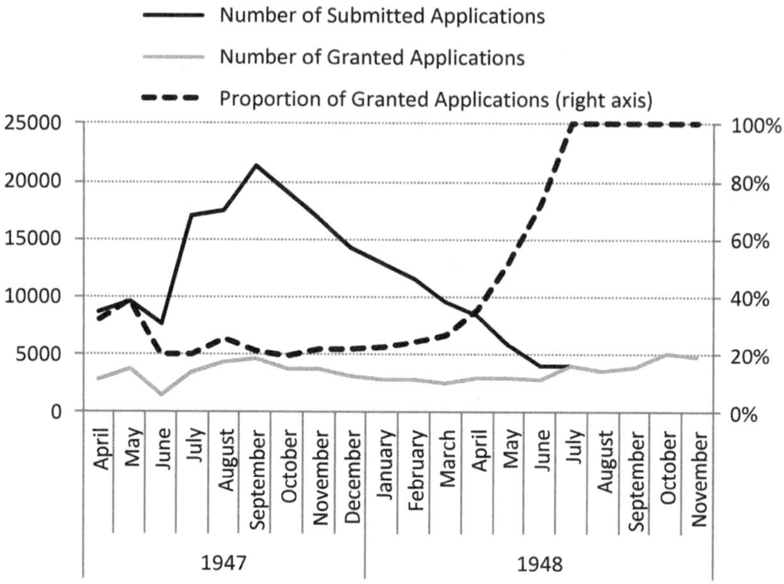

Fig. 2.2 Numbers of submitted and granted applications for new construction based on temporary regulations on the restriction of construction, Tokyo (*Source*: Tokyo-to Kenchiku-kyoku [The Tokyo Metropolitan Government, Construction Bureau], *Shidō-ka Jigyōgaiyō* [The Guidance Division Business Outline] (1954): p. 15)

construction and building materials, which was reinforced in 1946 and 1947, was among the crucial factors that constrained the creation of living spaces.

The number of completed houses began to decline in 1948. As shown in Fig. 2.2, the number of applications submitted for the construction of new houses and the number of cases in which an allotment of building materials was granted became identical in July 1948, and remained so thereafter. It was the tightening supply-demand balance of funds that subdued the demand for material to construct new houses. The supply-demand balance in building materials having slackened, the Regulations on the Allotment of Specified Production Materials were relaxed in June 1948. In 1949, the actual construction costs of wooden buildings started to fall below the official price levels. The controls on the distribution of building materials were no longer justified. In December 1949, the cabinet approved 'On the Matter of the Abolition of Unnecessary Regulations,' and controls on wood materials were lifted in January 1950. In November the same year, the Temporary Regulations on the Restriction of Construction were also removed. As has been explained, the controls on construction and the distribution of building materials were reinforced after having been relaxed immediately after the end of the war. Then, as the supply-demand balance with respect to building materials slackened, government control was gradually abolished. The removal of the controls on construction and building materials meant that constraints on housing construction, in the form of materials shortages, faded away.

3.2 *Financial Limitations*

3.2.1 Methods of Procuring Construction Funds

This section examines the second element that determined the private sector's self-funded reconstruction activities: the methods by which construction funds were procured. In the late 1940s, which corresponds to the period between the end of the war and the establishment of the Housing Loan Corporation, the main sources of housing funds were: (1) the Deposit Bureau of the Ministry of Finance and government subsidies; (2) the Reconstruction Finance Corporation; (3) general financial institutions; and (4) self-funding by house owners/builders.

First, regarding the Deposit Bureau's funds, housing loans were made through the Nihon Kangyō Bank (The Industrial Bank of Japan) according to the 'Guidelines on Loans to Rent-house Associations and Housing Associations (including Joint Associations)' and 'Guidelines on Special Housing Reconstruction Loans to Individuals.' The purpose of these loans was to provide people who had lost their houses and housing associations in war-damaged areas with the funds necessary for the purchase or construction of houses up to 10,000 yen per household. This financial scheme, however, did not produce the expected results on account of the depletion of the Deposit Bureau's funds (Tokyo Shiseichōsakai Tokyo-to Sōmu-bu Chōsa-ka 1947, p. 24). In the case of government subsidies, it was decided that half the funds needed by local governments for the construction of prefabricated houses would be subsidized in line with the War Damage Reconstruction Agency's notification, 'Guidelines on Government Subsidy for Emergency Measures for Housing in War-damaged Cities,' issued on 22 November, 1945. In addition, half the funds necessary for the construction of low-rent public housing ('planned housing') designed to accommodate war repatriates and those who had been bombed out of their homes continued to be subsidized during and after fiscal 1946 (Kenchiku-kyoku Jūtaku-ka 1946b, pp. 38–39). In Tokyo, a total of 1,545,800 thousand yen subsidized the construction of about 10,000 prefabricated houses and about 23,000 'planned houses' during fiscal 1945 and between fiscal 1946 and 1948, respectively (Tokyo Shōkōkaigisho, February 1949b, p. 9). It is true that low-rent public housing projects financed through the half-the-cost subsidy system played a socially significant role, given the historical circumstances in which adequate rental-house supply could not be expected from the private sector of the economy. However, the housing budget accounted for only 0.42% of the government's total budgets between 1945 and 1949 (Kensetsu-shō Jūtaku-kyoku 1965, p. 17). As far as budget allotments were concerned, housing problem countermeasures ranked low among the government's policy priorities.

Next, let us examine the role played by the Reconstruction Finance Corporation in housing construction related to the coal-mining industry, the largest borrower from the Corporation. As of 31 March 1949, the total loans made by the Corporation to the coal-mining industry came to 47,520 million yen. Of that amount, 15,280 million yen was spent on housing construction for coal miners (Fukkō Kinyūkōko 1950, p. 55). As discussed further below, this amount is slightly larger than the estimated construction investment amount made in Tokyo between the end of the war and December 1948. It is also around ten times the total amount of government subsidies granted for the construction of 'planned housing' by the end of fiscal 1948. In contrast to the government's measures for addressing the housing problems of those who had lost their homes during the war, the housing construction for coal miners financed by the Reconstruction Finance Corporation was carried out fairly actively. However, the Corporation's housing loans were significant only as a means to achieving the ultimate purpose, which was to enhance production. They played only a limited role in contributing to post-war housing reconstruction (Matsuda 1949, pp. 35–36).

3.2.2 Self-Funded Housing Construction

It is estimated that 15,225 million yen was invested in construction work in Tokyo between August 1945 and December 1948. Of this amount, however, only 1680 million yen was financed by government subsidies and bonds. In other words, around 90% of construction investments were funded by the private sector (Tokyo Shōkōkaigisho, February 1949b, p. 5). Private-sector finance consisted mainly of loans by private financial institutions and of self-funding by house owners and builders. In the former case, long-term, low-interest loans for housing construction were almost non-existent at the time on account of the rapidly accelerating inflation (Tokyo Shiseichōsakai Tokyo-to Sōmu-bu Chōsa-ka 1947, p. 22). It can be assumed, therefore, that most of the private sector funding, which accounted for 90% of total construction investment in Tokyo during the post-war reconstruction period, was self-funded by house owners/builders.

Emergency financial measures implemented in February 1946, affected this process of self-funded housing construction in a crucial way. The Emergency Financial Measures Ordinance set an upper limit on the amount of cash that could be withdrawn from a bank account. People were thus forced to live what was dubbed 'the 500-yen life.' In principle, withdrawals of up to 5000 yen from bank accounts was permitted for housing funds. In reality, however, it was almost impossible to build even a prefabricated house with 5000 yen. The maximums on cash withdrawals were raised gradually, as inflation escalated. However, the revised limits remained far below actual construction costs. Under these circumstances, the only people able to accumulate enough cash to build or purchase a house were those belonging to the so-called 'new yen class,' which consisted mainly of those engaged in the materials trade or the service industry. An inquiry into Tokyo metropolitan area new-house construction during the period in question showed that owners who completed a house construction were, in many cases, engaged in occupations relatively advantageous for the accumulation of the new yen: for instance, traders in food products, restaurant owners, and brokers and employees of companies dealing with building materials (Usui et al. 1947, p. 5). Because construction costs rose more rapidly than the maximum amount of cash withdrawal permitted, houses were hardly affordable except for those who had access to the new yen (Itō 1946, p. 20).

Because of the building materials shortage and the financial limitations on housing construction, the proportion of construction investments to GNP dropped from 3.4% to 2.4% between 1935 and 1947 (Tokyo Shōkōkaigisho, January 1949a, p. 6). According to a written opinion submitted by the Tokyo Chamber of Commerce and Industry in December 1948, the largest obstacle to housing reconstruction was the lack of funds, whereas the shortage of building materials was being mitigated. Between the end of the war and the first half of fiscal 1947, an annual average of about 500,000 houses was constructed around the country, the maximum possible number in terms of the availability of building materials. This indicates that there were millions of people around the country with sufficient resources to be a source of effective demand for housing. It follows that most of the people who did not have their own houses at the end of 1948 were those without sufficient funds to build them by themselves (Kensetsu-shō Jūtaku-kyoku 1949).

The class of those who had suffered war damage but who were able to accumulate sufficient cash – that is, the 'new yen class' – was able to escape from the social stratum of the houseless. For the remainder who did not possess enough funds, however, the dissipation of the materials shortage did not lead to their building their own houses. What they really wanted was the kind of rented houses they had used to live in. Given the rent control then being enforced, however, they had little chance to regain them. In reality, their demand for living spaces was met by a redistribution of existing living spaces in the form of room-renting, which became a widespread practice in all social classes. The government's housing budgets were too small, relative to the actual shortage. Since it was practically impossible for an ordinary worker to build a house with his own money, the need to provide long-term, low-interest housing loans was strongly felt among the general public (Hori 1948, p. 5). Eventually, this matter was discussed in the Housing Council, leading to the establishment of the Housing Loan Corporation in 1950.

3.3 *Structural Changes in the Housing Land Market*

3.3.1 The Ownership and Utilization of Housing Land

This section examines the third determinant of self-funded construction activities by those in the private sector: that is, the ownership and utilization of housing land. Table 2.5 shows areas and ownership concentration of Tokyo metropolitan area housing land on 15 July 1947. Although the table does not include numbers on absentee landowners, it reflects the research results on 13,000 parcels of land. It is useful, therefore, for the purpose of gaining an overall view of the land-ownership structure in Tokyo in the immediate post-war period. Large landowners with more than 1000 *tsubo* (approximately 3305 m^2) of housing land accounted for 11.6% of the total number of landowners. In terms of area, they owned 65.3% of total housing land. Landowners with more than 100 *tsubo* (approximately 330.5 m^2) and less than 300 *tsubo* (approximately 991.7 m^2) of housing land accounted for 37.3% of

Table 2.5 Numbers of landowners by area of owned land and purpose of land use, Tokyo (15 July, 1947)

Area of owned land (tsubo: 3.3 m^2)	Number of landowners (Proportion)		Total area (tsubo) (a) (Proportion)		Purpose of land use (tsubo)			b/a
					Used by the owners (b)	Leased	Others	
Less than 50 Tsubo	266	14.9%	9328	0.9%	6581	1997	750	70.6%
50–100 Tsubo	308	17.2%	25,194	2.5%	17,155	5329	2710	68.1%
100–300 Tsubo	667	37.3%	125,626	12.5%	86,434	29,509	9683	68.8%
300–1000 Tsubo	339	19.0%	189,295	18.8%	100,695	75,506	13,094	53.2%
1000–5000 Tsubo	179	10.0%	389,690	38.7%	88,131	275,426	26,133	22.6%
More than 5000 Tsubo	29	1.6%	267,023	26.5%	42,777	209,989	14,257	16.0%
Total	1788	100.0%	1,006,156	100.0%	341,773	597,756	66,627	34.0%

Source: Kensetsu-shō Kenchiku-kyoku Jūtakukikaku-ka [The Ministry of Construction, Construction Bureau, Housing Planning Section] *Shōwa 22 Nendo Takuchi Chōsakekka* [The Results of the Survey on Housing Lands, Fiscal 1947] (1948): pp. 139–145

total landowners. In terms of area, however, they owned only 12.5%. Small landowners with less than 50 *tsubo* (approximately 165.3 m^2) of housing land made up 12.5% of the total number of landowners, while possessing less than 1% of total housing land.

Next, these data need to be compared with those of the pre-war period. According to a study of the 1912 land ownership structure in the fifteen wards that then constituted Tokyo City, large landowners with more than 1000 *tsubo* of land accounted for 9.0% of the total number of landowners and 67.8% of total housing land (Nomura 1998, pp. 164–165). Because the data do not include the figures for that five rural districts that merged with the fifteen wards in 1932, a comparison with Table 2.5 has to be made with care. Nevertheless, it is evident that the basic structure in which the top 10% of landowners possessed more than half the total housing land remained almost unchanged from 1912 through July 1947. According to another study of three Tokyo districts, however, ownership of 48% of the total number of land parcels was transferred during the 4 years between August 1945 and July 1949 (Tokyodaigaku Shakaikagaku Kenkyūsho 1952, p. 38). In short, although the land ownership structure hardly changed on the surface, a large number of landowners were replaced in the afternoon the war. A growing number of landowners sold off their land or paid taxes in kind, because of the tax hikes on real property, while people belonging to the 'new yen class' purchased housing land for their own use.

As shown in Table 2.5, landowners with less than 300 *tsubo* of land used about 70% of their land for their own purposes (mostly for dwelling or business) and leased the remainder. This class of landowners constituted the core of the social stratum of real property owners when it came to land. Landowners with more than 1000 *tsubo*, by contrast, leased for more land than they used for their own purposes. In the Tokyo metropolitan area, leased land accounted for 60% of the total housing area, most of it supplied by this class of large landowners. Meanwhile, the proportion of owned houses in the Tokyo metropolitan area was 47.4% as of July 1947. Of these, 79.8% were on leased lands (Kensetsu-shō Kenchiku-kyoku Jūtakukikaku-ka 1948, pp. 5–12). In addition, fully 41% of leased lands had leasehold contracts that had been newly made during the two-and-a-half years between 1945 and July 1947 (Ibid., pp. 102–104). This indicates that leasehold rights were eagerly sought after in the early postwar years. According to an inquiry into leasehold contracts in three areas in Tokyo, the proportion of leasehold contracts made after the end of the war were much higher in war-damaged districts than in unaffected districts. Moreover, in war-damaged districts, there was turnover in most of the tenants after the war (Tokyo Daigaku Shakaikagaku Kenkyūsho, 1952, p. 52). Demand for leased land grew in step with post-war reconstruction and its utilization was especially pronounced in war-damaged areas. Among the institutional factors contributing to the acceleration of this utilization of leased lands was the enactment of the Act on Temporary Measures Concerning Land and House Leasing in War-damaged Cities.

3.3.2 The Utilization of Leased Lands

The Wartime Damaged Lands and Buildings Ordinance (Imperial Ordinance No. 411) was issued in July 1945 in order to address the complicated leasehold relationships in war-stricken cities. It thereby became legally possible for tenants of war-damaged properties to use leased lands to construct provisional buildings without the consent of the landowners or land leaseholders (Saikōsaibansho Jimukyoku Minji-bu 1947, pp. 51–56). In September 1946, the Act on Temporary Measures Concerning Leased Lands and Buildings in War-damaged Cities (hereafter referred to as the War-damage Act) was put into effect. It guaranteed the continuation of land leasehold rights in cases where tenants' buildings had been burned down during the war. It also gave tenants of war-damaged buildings the highest precedence in the following contracts: (1) land leasehold rights in cases where they did not have one; (2) land purchases in case where they already had land leasehold rights; and (3) house leasehold rights in cases where that damaged buildings were to be reconstructed. Landowners and leaseholders were not allowed to reject the tenants' propositions without justification. The purpose of the War Damage Act was to encourage the construction of provisional buildings on war-damaged sites and to guarantee, for a certain period of time, continuous land use to those who were actually using the lands after the abolition of the Wartime Damaged Lands and Buildings Ordinance. The Act sought to help actual land users acquire land leasehold rights and to provide war survivors with a stable living situation (Kizokuin 1946, p. 14). Among the people who suffered damage from the war, those with the will and the money to construct new houses were given opportunities to obtain land leasehold rights. At the same time, protection was given to those without sufficient funds through provision (3) mentioned above (Saikōsaibansho Jimukyoku Minji-bu 1947, p. 2). In reality, however, it was unlikely that landowners or land leaseholders whose rental houses had been damaged during the war would construct new houses again on the same sites and rent them to the same tenants. In practice, therefore, the main purpose of the War Damage Act was to give tenants with resources precedence in land leasehold rights so that they could construct new houses of their own (Sakamoto 1949, p. 39).

While tenants with sufficient funds enjoyed institutional support from the War Damage Act, the leasehold rights acquisition problem for those lacking in funds remained unresolved (Tokyo Shiseichōsakai Tokyo-to Sōmu-bu Chōsa-ka 1947, p. 29). According to a survey of new house owners who completed their houses in April 1947, the largest proportion were land leaseholders who had held their rights since the pre-war period: 48.8% (Ibid., p. 30). The next largest class of new house owners was composed of former tenants who acquired land leasehold rights thanks to the War Damage Act: 19.0%. By contrast, only 12.4% were landowners who constructed new houses. It can be assumed that those who answered ‘Others’ in the survey (20.1%) included many third-party people who had obtained land leasehold rights. Public consultation and mediation services concerning leased lands and houses based on the War Damage Act were provided, with Tokyo’s local government offices providing consultation in 32,847 cases (38.4% of the total number of consultation cases nationwide) between September 1946 and March 1948 (Fukkōkyoku Chisei-ka, 1948). Of these, 14,298 cases (43.5%) were consultations from land leaseholders and 11,138 (33.9%) from tenants. Although the acquisition of land leasehold rights was spurred by the War Damage Act, many people in war-damaged cities were still living in air-raid shelters or provisional huts, doing nothing about the lands on which they were dwelling. Therefore, attempts were made to inform the general public about the War Damage Act by means of radios, newspapers, magazines, public posters and so on.

The utilization of leased lands led to a rise in land leasehold prices. For example, in what was then Shitaya Ward, land leasehold prices rose 1.3 to 2.2 times from 1948 through 1949 (Tokyo-to 1948, 1949). The price increases were higher than those of lands with leasehold interests. Land leasehold prices came to 80–90% of the price of land with leasehold interests in the case of commercial real estate, and around 50% in the case of housing land. The rise in land leasehold prices reflected the growing demand for leased lands. While the ‘new yen class’ began to acquire leasehold rights on commercial properties, the acquisition of leasehold rights by those without sufficient funds progressed only slowly (Sakamoto 1949, p. 39). While the War Damage Act weakened the rights of traditional landowners relatively speaking, land leaseholders with assets enjoyed protection and former tenants who had sufficient resources became able to obtain land leasehold rights. It was these comparatively well-to-do land leaseholders and former tenants who played the key role in the self-funded reconstruction activities in war-damaged cities. By contrast, those who suffered war damage and did not have sufficient funds had no choice but to depend on their personal connections in the hope of benefitting from the redistribution of existing living spaces, namely, from the renting of rooms in houses that had survived the war.

4 Conclusion

This study did not adopt the conventional investigative framework, which views the war-induced housing shortage as a continuation of the pre-war peacetime housing shortage problem. Instead, it has conceived of it as a problem with a historical structure specific to the period differing from both the preceding and the following periods. Once government controls were introduced, houses stopped being supplied as "commodities" for distribution through market mechanisms. Living spaces were nevertheless indispensable for people's existence and for the expansion of the labor force, and were thus 'de-commodified,' such that they were created and distributed as 'lived spaces.' This study has analyzed this process with a comprehensive examination of the disruption of the supply system and the changes in ownership structure. It has attempted thereby to highlight the aspects of post-war reconstruction that traditional historiography, focused mainly on institutional factors such as city planning, has failed to grasp. The above investigation is summarized as follows.

Government controls both during and after the war destroyed the housing supply structure that had been established during the interwar period and created a structure specific to the control years. The rent control on houses during the war was intended to stabilize prices while encouraging the rental house supply, even though, in practice, it led to the stagnation of investment in the house-renting business. Separately, the housing rent controls of the post-war reconstruction period mainly served to protect the tenants of rented houses that had escaped destruction during the war, although the ostensible policy objective was to stabilize people's living situations more generally. Policy makers were well aware that rent control would destroy the existing housing supply system. The tenants who gained by it did so as the direct outcome of traditional house owners' economic losses. It can also be said that the sought-for 'stability' was brought about, in indirect ways, by the unstable living conditions of war those who had suffered war damage in general. That is, the housing standards of rented houses eventually deteriorated significantly. The maintenance of rent control on houses after the war, along with heavy taxation, precipitated the change in the ownership structure of rented houses. An increasing number of them were turned into owned houses.

This change in the ownership structure, which was forced by post-war regulations and reforms, occurred simultaneously with the creation of 'de-commodified' living spaces. The formation of these post-war living spaces proceeded from the emergency stage of utilizing air-raid shelters and provisional huts to the new stage in which survivors of wartime damage made self-funded reconstruction efforts. Wood materials were procured through various unofficial routes, bypassing government regulations. The 'new yen class,' comprising those with personal connections and sufficient funds to purchase materials on the black market, was the driving force in such activities. The two major factors that crucially affected the supply of wood immediately after the end of the war were the government's control on construction and building materials and the Occupation Forces' housing demand. As the gap between official and actual wood prices narrowed during and after 1948, due to the stagnation of new housing construction, controls on construction and building materials were gradually removed. New housing construction was the result of a funding shortage. At this point, the determining factor in the private sector's self-help reconstruction activities was no longer the shortage of materials but the constraint on finances. Before the establishment of the Housing Loan Corporation, housing construction in war-damaged cities was mainly self-funded. With the tightening of the supply-demand balance in housing funds because of the combination of the Emergency Financial Measures Ordinance and rapid inflation, the procurement of housing funds became more and more difficult. In this environment, it was the 'new yen class' that was able to accumulate sufficient funds. By the final stages of the control period, those who had suffered war damage and who had sufficient funds had already escaped the class of the destitute who did not have stability in housing. For those who lost their dwellings to war damage and remained without sufficient funds, on the other hand, the dissipation of the materials shortage did not enable them to construct new houses. Although what they wanted was rental houses, they had little chance of finding them because the rental house supply structure of the interwar period had been demolished. They therefore had no choice but to depend on the redistribution of existing living spaces in the form of room-renting through personal connections. Room-renting became a widespread practice in all social classes.

Around 80% of owned houses in the Tokyo metropolitan area stood on leased lands in 1947. In addition, more than 40% of the leased lands had been acquired by new owners immediately after the end of the war. The utilization of leased lands proceeded as the post-war reconstruction intensified the demand for leased lands. Among the institutional factors behind this trend was the enactment of the Act on Temporary Measures Concerning Land and House Leasing in War-damaged Cities. On the basis of this Act, measures were taken that somewhat weakened traditional landownership. At the same time, wealthy land leaseholders were given protection and wealthy former tenants became able to acquire land leasehold rights more easily. Land leaseholders and former tenants with sufficient funds were the driving force in the private sector's self-funded reconstruction activities in war-damaged cities. At the same time, the redistribution of existing living spaces in the form of room-renting played a crucial role in the reconstruction process for a long period of time.

Wartime air raids divided city inhabitants into two categories: those whose houses were damaged and those whose houses were intact. For a full understanding of the wartime housing shortage, attention should be drawn to the extreme disparity between those who were burned out of their houses and those who retained them. Concerning the latter, there were two types: Type (1), a single household occupying the whole house; and Type (2), a household renting a room (or rooms) to another.

Among those who had lost their houses during the war, there were also two types: Type (3), rent-room tenants; and Type (4), those who constructed their own houses with their own funds. Type (2) and Type (3) combined to form a joint-household sharing the same house. The 'new yen class' constituted the core of Type (4) households. They were the only class of people able to satisfy the requirements for the basic elements of housing construction, namely building materials, funds and lands. Although they succeeded in escaping from the class of the destitute without houses, they lived in new spaces of such low quality that they fell into the category of 'deteriorated houses' after just a few years. In 1950, more than 40% of total households, including Type (2), were still sharing the same houses. This proportion was hardly lower than that of the period immediately after the war. An enormous number of people would not have been able to live in war-damaged cities without the room-renting arrangements enabled by personal connections. At the same time, however, the congestion of the living spaces and attrition of buildings considerably lowered the standard of Tokyo's housing. How to supply proper living spaces for tenants crammed into overcrowded rental rooms – in other words, how to cope with the problem of the 're-commodification' of living spaces – became a vexing theme of the government's post-war housing policy.

After the end of the war, the government invested materials and funds preferentially in industrial sectors of the economy, thus realizing economic recovery in a relatively short period of time. It was a recovery, however, that was carried out at the price of the devastation of the country's natural and urban environments (Keizaianteihonbu 1949, pp. 29–34). Contradictions in the recovery process accumulated most heavily in the housing sector, which constructed the foundation of people's daily lives. The flexible use of living spaces – multiple households living together in the same house – had been an important feature of the pre-war Japanese urban housing market, but it manifested itself most markedly and significantly during the post-war period of government controls, functioning as a crucial factor in the reconstruction process. This feature was to Japan's post-war reconstruction, which was in marked contrast with the experience of European countries, where public housing construction projects were the pillar of post-war reconstruction.

References

Arai, Haruji and Gan Nagai. 1946. *Zaisanzei no Kaisetsu* [Property Taxes Explained]. Tokyo: Yoshida Shobō.

Chūō Bukkatōsei Kyōryokukaigi Chōsa-bu (The Central Price Control Cooperation Council, Investigation Department). 1944. *Fudōsankakaku no Tōkijōkyō* [On the Rise in Real Estate Prices].

Fukkō Kin'yū Kōko (The Reconstruction Finance Corporation). 1950. *Fukukinyūshi no Kaiko* [Reconstruction Finance Memoirs].

Fukkō-kyoku Seichi-ka (The Reconstruction Agency, Site Preparation Section). 1946–1949. *Risaitoshi Shakuchi Shakuya Rinjishorihō ni kansuru Tsuzuri* [Bound Documents Pertaining to the Act on Temporary Measures Concerning Land and House Lease in War-damaged Cities].

Hatsuda, Kōsei. 2011. *Toshi no Sengo* [Cities in the Post-war Period], Tokyo: The University of Tokyo Press.
Honjō, Kazuhiko. 1948. Jūtakukeizai ni kansuru Tōkei ni tsuite [On Housing Statistics]. *Kenchikuzasshi* (Architecture Journal) 737.
Hori, Hitoyuki. 1948. Jūtakumondai Kaiketsu no Konponsaku [The Fundamental Solution to Housing Problems]. *Jitsugyō no Sekai* [Business World] 45 (8).
Inoue, Makoto. 2012. *Shōdo karano Saisei* [Rebirth from the Ruins]. Tokyo: Shinchōsha.
Isahaya, Nobuo. 1946. Genka no Jūtaku Shoseisaku [Current Housing Policies]. *Kenchikuzasshi* (The Architecture Journal) 726 and 727.
Ishida, Yorifusa. 1991. *Tokyo Toshikeikaku Monogatari* [The Story of Tokyo's City Planning]. Tokyo: Nihon Keizai Hyōronsha.
Itō, Kazuhiko. 1946. Sensaifukkō – Tokuni Jūtaku no Fukkō ni kansuru Shokan [Personal Impressions About the Reconstruction from the War Damage, Especially the Housing Reconstruction]. *Fukkōjōhō* (Information on Reconstruction) 2 (8).
Jūtaku Kin'yū Kōko (The Housing Loan Corporation). 1960. *Jūtaku Kin'yū Kōko Nijūnenshi* [The Twenty-Year History of the Housing Loan Corporation].
Jūtakukikaku-ka (The Housing Planning Division). 1946. Kiro ni Tatsu Genkō Chidai Yachin Tōseirei [Current Land and House Rent Regulations at a Crossroads]. *Fukkōjōhō* [Information on Reconstruction] 2 (2).
Keizaianteihonbu (The Economic Stabilization Agency). 1949. *Keizai no Genkyō Bunseki* [The Analysis of the Current State of the Economy].
Kenchiku-kyoku Jūtaku-ka (The Construction Agency, Housing Section). 1946a. Shōwa 21 Nen 3 Gatsumatsu ni okeru Jūtaku no Fukkōjōkyō [The State of Housing Reconstruction at the End of March, 1946]. *Fukkōjōhō* [Information on Reconstruction] 2 (7).
———. 1946b. Shōwa 21 Nendo Daiichiji Jūtakukankei Kokkohojo [The First State Subsidies for Housing in Fiscal 1946]. *Fukkōjōhō* [Information on Reconstruction] 2 (10).
Kenchiku-kyoku Kantoku-ka (The Construction Agency, Supervising Section). 1946. Rinji Kenchikuseigenrei no Shikō ni tsuite [On the Implementation of the Temporary Building Restrictions Ordinance]. *Fukkōjōhō* [Information on Reconstruction] 2 (6).
Kensetsu-shō Jūtaku-kyoku (The Ministry of Construction, Housing Bureau). 1949. *Jūtakumondai Taisakusiryō Tsuzuri* [Bound Documents on Countermeasures to Housing Problems].
———. 1951. *Jūtakunenkan* (Housing Yearbook). Tokyo: Shōkokusha.
———. 1953. *Yachin Yanushi Jittaichōsa Kekkahōkokusho* [Report of the Results of the Survey on the Actual State of House Rents and Owners].
———. 1965. *Jūtakutaisaku Yōran, Shōwa 40 Nendoban* [Outline of Countermeasures to Housing Problems, Fiscal 1965]. Nihon: Jūtakukyōkai [Japan Housing Association].
Kensetsu-shō Kenchiku-kyoku Jūtakukikaku-ka (The Ministry of Construction, Construction Bureau, Housing Planning Section). 1948. *Shōwa 22 Nendo Takuchi Chōsakekka* [The Results of the Survey on Housing Lands, Fiscal 1947].
Kizokuin (The House of Peers). 1946. *Risaitoshi Shakuchi Shakuya Rinjishorihōan Tokubetsuiinkai Gijisokkiroku* [Stenographic Records of the Proceedings of the Special Committee for the Bill on Temporary Measures Concerning Land and House Leasing in War-damaged Cities] 1.
Koizumi, Kazuko, Akira Takayabu, and Seizō Uchida. 1999. *Senryōgun Jūtaku no Kiroku (Jō)* [Records of the Occupation Forces' Housing 1]. Tokyo: Sumaino Toshokan Shuppankyoku.
Kōsei-shō Jūtaku-kyoku (The Ministry of Welfare, Housing Bureau). 1942. *Daitoshi Jūtakuchōsa Tōkeihyō* [Statistical Tables of the Survey on Housing in Large Cities].
Koshizawa, Akira. 1991. *Tokyo no Toshikeikaku* (Tokyo's City Planning). Tokyo: Iwanami Shoten.
Matsuda, Kunimitsu. 1949. Genzai ni okeru Jūtakukin'yū no Mondaiten [Problems with the Current Housing Finance]. *Keizaiantei Shiryō* [Documents on Economic Stabilization] 8.
Narita, Ryūichi. 2003. *Kindai Toshikūkan no Bunkakeiken* [The Cultural Experience of Modern Urban Space]. Tokyo: Iwanami Shoten.
Nishiyama, Uzō. 1942. *Jūtaku Mondai* [Housing Problems]. Tokyo: Sagami Shobō.
———. 1952. *Nihon no Jūtaku Mondai* [Housing Problems in Japan]. Tokyo: Iwanami Shoten.

———. 1989. *Sumai Kōkongaku* [Today's Housing Conditions]. Tokyo: Shōkokusha.

Nomura, Etsuko. 1998. Meiji 45 Nen no Chisekidaichō no Bunseki ni yoru Takuchi Shoyūkeitai no Ruikeika [Typification of the Housing Land Ownership Structures Based on the Analysis of the 1912 Cadaster]. *Nihon Kenchiku Gakkai Keikakukei Ronbunshū* [Collected Papers of the Architectural Institute of Japan, the Planning Division] 504.

Nōrinsuisan Shizai Juyōshadantai Kyōgikai (The Agriculture, Forestry and Fishery Material Consumers' Council). 1947. *Kaiteizōhoban Shitei Seisanshizai Kankeihōki to Kaisetsu* [Laws and Regulations Related to Specified Production Materials and Their Explanations: Revised and Enlarged Edition].

Saikōsaibansho Jimukyoku Minji-bu (The Supreme Court, Secretariat, Civil Case Department). 1947. *Kaisei Risaitoshi Shakuchi Shakuya Rinjishorihō ni tsuite* [On the Amendment of the Act on Temporary Measures Concerning Land and House Leasing in War-damaged Cities].

Saitō, Itsurō. 1946. Chidai Yachin Tōseirei no Gaiyō [Outline of the Land and House Rent Control Ordinance]. *Fukkōjōhō* [Information on Reconstruction] 2 (11).

Saitō, Shin'ichi. 1948. Itō Kyokuchō ni Jūtakumondai wo Kiku [Ask Director Itō About the Housing Problem]. *Gekkan Zaimoku* [Monthly Wood Journal] 8 (8).

Sakamoto, Etsuo. 1949. Risaitoshi Shakuchi Shakuya Rinjishorihō to Sono Un'yō [The Act on Temporary Measures concerning Land and House Lease in War-Damaged Cities and Its Implementation]. *Hanrei Taimuzu* [The Journal of Judicial Precedents] 5.

Sensai Fukkōin (The War Damage Reconstruction Agency). 1945. Risaitoshi Kinkyū Jūtakutaisakuhi ni taisuru Kokkohojo [State Subsidies for the Expenses of the Emergency Countermeasures against Housing Problems in War-damaged Cities]. *Fukkōjōhō* [Information on Reconstruction] 1.

———. 1946a. Shōwa 21 Nendo Daiichiji Jūtakutaisaku Yōkōan [A Plan for the Outline of the First Countermeasures against Housing Problems, Fiscal 1946]. *Shidehara Naikaku Jikankaigi Shorui* [Documents on the Shidehara Government Vice-ministers' Meetings] 2.

———. 1946b. Kin'yū Kinkyūsochirei Kōfuka ni okeru Jūtakusonota no Kenchikushikin [Construction Costs of Houses and Other Buildings Under the Emergency Financial Measures Ordinance]. *Fukkōjōhō* [Information on Reconstruction] 2 (4).

Sensai Fukkōin Kenchiku-kyoku Kantoku-ka (The War Damage Reconstruction Agency, Construction Bureau, Supervising Section). 1957. *Kenchikukyoka to Shizaiwariate* [Building Permit and Materials Allotment].

Shinrinshigen Sōgōtaisaku Kyōgikai (The Comprehensive Forest Resources Countermeasures Council). 1951. *Mokuzai no Jukyū* [The Supply and Demand for Wood].

Shōkō-shō (The Ministry of Commerce and Industry). 1946. Shinchūgun Jūtaku oyobi Heishatō Setsueiyōshizai ni kansuru Ken [In the Matter of Building Materials for the Housing and Barracks of the Occupation Forces]. In Naikaku Kanbō Naikaku Sanjikan Shitsu [The Cabinet Secretariat, Cabinet Counsellors' Office], *Shidehara Naikaku Kakugikettei Shorui* [Documents on Shidehara Government's Cabinet Decisions] 5.

Sōri-fu Tōkei-kyoku (The Prime Minister's Office, Statistics Bureau). 1954a. *Shōwa 25 Nen Kokuseichōsa Hōkoku* [Reports on the 1950 National Census] 4.

———. 1954b. *Shōwa 28 Nen Jūtaku Tōkeichōsa Kekkahōkoku* [Reports on the Results of the 1953 Statistical Survey on Housing].

Tani, Shigeo. 1950. *Chidai Yachin Tōsei no Kaisetsu* [Explanation of Land and House Rent Controls]. Tokyo: Jijitsūshinsha.

Tiratsoo, Nick, Takao Matsumura, Tony Mason, and Jun'ichi Hasegawa. 2006. *Sensaifukkō no Nichieihikaku* [War Damage Reconstruction: A Comparison Between Japan and the UK]. Tokyo: Chisen Shokan.

Tokyo Shiseichōsakai Tokyo-to Sōmu-bu Chōsa-ka (The Tokyo Municipal Administration Investigation Council and the Tokyo Metropolitan Government, General Affairs Department, Investigation Section). 1947. *Tokyo-to no Jūtakumondai ni kansuru Chōsahōkoku* [Reports on the Results of the Survey of Housing Problems in the Tokyo Metropolitan Area].

Tokyo Shōkōkaigisho (The Tokyo Chamber of Commerce and Industry). 1949a. Jūtakushikin Taisaku ni tsuite [On Financial Measures for Housing]. *Tōshōjihō* [The Tokyo Chamber of Commerce and Industry News] 22.

———. 1949b. Jūtakushikin no Shomondai [Problems Concerning Housing Finance]. *Chōsashiryō* [Survey Documents] 1.

Tokyodaigaku Shakaikagaku Kenkyūsho (The Institute of Social Science, the University of Tokyo). 1952. *Sengo Takuchi Jūtaku no Jittai [The Actual State of Housing Lands and Houses in the Post-war Period]*. Tokyo: The University of Tokyo Press.

———. 1953. *Nihonshakai no Jūtakumondai* [Housing Problems in Japanese Society]. Tokyo: The University of Tokyo Press.

Tokyo-to (The Tokyo Metropolitan Government). 1948. *Takuchikakaku Chōsahyō: Shōwa 23 Nen 3 Gatsu 1 Nichi Genzai* [Tables of the Housing Land Price Survey, as of 1 March, 1948].

———. 1949. *Shōwa 24 Nendo Takuchikakaku Chōsahyō* [Tables of the Housing Land Price Survey, Fiscal 1949].

———. 1953. *Tokyo-to Sensaishi* [Records of War Damages in Tokyo].

Tokyo-to Kenchiku-ka (The Tokyo Metropolitan Government, Building Section). 1946. *Fukkō Shominkenchiku no Genjō* [The Current State of Reconstruction: People's Building Activities].

Tokyo-to Sōmu-bu Tōkei-ka (The Tokyo Metropolitan Government, General Affairs Department, Statistics Section). 1947. *Tokyo-to Tōkeihyō: Kakei Bukka Hen* (The Tokyo Metropolitan Government Statistical Tables: Household Expenses and Prices).

Tokyo-to Sōmu-kyoku Tōkei-bu (The Tokyo Metropolitan Government, General Affairs Bureau, Statistics Department). 1945a. Sōsoku ni Kaiketsu Shitai Sensaisha no Jūtaku [The Housing Problem of Those Who Suffered War Damage Need to be Solved Immediately]. *Asahi Shimbun* [The Asahi Newspaper] 13 June 1945.

———. 1945b. Mokuzaiidō wo Jiyū ni Kigyōkyokasei mo Teppai [Free Wood Circulation Needed and the Corporation License System Be Abolished]. *Asahi Shimbun* 27 November 1945.

———. 1946a. Jūtaku Fukkyūshikin Kangin nite Yūzūkaishi [Funds for Housing Reconstruction Have Just Started to Be Financed through the Nihon Kangyō Bank]. *Fukkōjōhō* (Information on Reconstruction) 2 (1).

———. 1946b–1948. *Sengoshoki ni okeru Mokuzai Jukyū Kakaku Kanrenshiryō* [Documents on the Supply and Demand for Wood and Its Prices in the Early Stages of the Post-war Period].

———. 1955. *Tokyo-to no Jinkō ni kansuru Tōkeishiryō* [Statistical Data on the Population of the Tokyo Metropolitan Area].

Usui, Ken'ichi, Kunio Kawagoe, and Kō Irisawa. 1947. Jūtaku oyobi Tenpo no Fukkō ni kansuru Jitsujōchōsa [Survey on the Actual State of Commercial and Housing Reconstruction]. *Sensai Fukkōin Gijutsukenkyūsho Yōhō* [The War Damage Reconstruction Agency Technology Research Institute Journal] 2.

Watari, Kario. 1948. Waga Toshi no Jūtakufukkō o Kataru [About the Housing Reconstruction of My City]. *Shinjūtaku* [The New Housing] 14.

Chapter 3
Communal Unemployment Insurance in Wilhelminian Germany: A Case Study of the Greater Berlin Administration Union

Takahito Mori

Abstract In Wilhelminian Germany, unemployment insurance was introduced at the end of the nineteenth century at the communal level, but not at the national level. The main system of communal unemployment insurance was the Genter system, under which municipalities paid subsidies to trade unions that provided their out-of-work members with unemployment benefits. The system suffered from two problems: the exclusion of non-organized labourers, who comprised the majority of the working class, and the increase in the influence of the Social Democratic Party. This occurred because the Genter system provided financial support for the Free Trade Union under the influence of the Party. Despite these problems, however, the introduction of the Genter system was considered in many municipalities, such as Schöneberg and Charlottenburg in the Greater Berlin administration union. The municipality of Schöneberg successfully established a system based on the Genter system that aimed to include non-organized labourers. A similar system was proposed in Charlottenburg, but was rejected by the city council. The objective of this article is to provide a comparative analysis of both municipalities and to show the historical context of the Genter system with a focus on 'the social task of municipalities', a topic of interest in political philosophy at that time.

Keywords Genter system • Social liberalism • The 'social task of the municipality' • Greater Berlin • Schöneberg • Charlottenburg

---

This chapter is a translation of an article that originally appeared in *Shakai Keizai Shigaku* 77(1) (May 2011), pp. 71–91.

T. Mori (✉)
Graduate School of Economics, Hitotsubashi University,
Naka 2-1, Kunitachi, Tokyo 186-8601, Japan
e-mail: tmori@econ.hit-u.ac.jp

S. Baba (ed.), *Economic History of Cities and Housing*, Monograph Series of the Socio-Economic History Society, Japan, DOI 10.1007/978-981-10-4097-9_3

1 Introduction

As a pioneer of social insurance at the national level, the German Reich (Second German Empire) introduced three social insurance plans in the 1880s: health insurance, insurance for injuries at work and old-age pensions. Conversely, Germany lagged behind other countries in unemployment insurance, which was not introduced at a national level until 1927, while in Britain, for example, it was already in place before World War I (Ritter 1989). The main reason was that even though unemployment had been counted as an acute social risk ever since the "Great Depression" of the 1870s, the need for unemployment insurance did not receive wide recognition because the average unemployment rate stayed at around 2% from 1895 to 1913 (Faust 1986; Ritter and Tenfelde 1992). Recent research shows, however, that unemployment statistics were limited and thus did not contain accurate information about the real situation. This was especially true for cities, where seasonal labourers such as construction workers were often faced with the risk of unemployment. Unemployment became a serious problem for such workers during any period of depression (Fukuzawa 2007).[1]

In this context, German municipalities began to develop their own policies to deal with unemployment in addition to their traditional poor relief programmes. Firstly, from the end of the 1880s, they adopted *Krisenarbeit* (emergency relief programmes) to create jobs such as wood chopping and macadam making for the unemployed during the winter. Secondly, from the 1890s employment offices were municipalized, and managed jointly by employers and employees (Krabbe 1981). Besides these efforts, some municipalities tried to introduce unemployment insurance. The pioneer was the municipality of Cologne, which set up a scheme for 'insurance against winter unemployment' in 1896, to protect seasonal labourers (Faust 1986). However, this system was not followed by other municipalities, and the main system to be adopted was the Genter system, which had been devised in Ghent (Gand), a Belgian city, in 1901. Municipalities that adopted this system paid subsidies to help trade unions to provide their out-of-work members with unemployment benefits.

The Genter system presupposed the existence of unemployment benefits paid by trade unions. This was one of the main forms of mutual aid organized by the trade unions, along with health and travel benefits, and its importance grew, especially from the 1890s. For example, in the Free Trade Union, the biggest alliance of trade unions in Germany which was under the influence of the Social Democratic Party, the percentage of members who had the right to request unemployment benefits increased from 13% in 1891 to 81% in 1913, while the amount of benefits paid in the same period rose, from 45,000 to 115.3 million Marks (Schönhoven 1980). The evolution of trade union unemployment benefits fostered the diffusion of the Genter

[1] Sixty percent of bricklayers, for example, were unemployed in the winter of 1908/1909, while 44% of construction workers were unemployed in the winter of 1911/1912 (Ritter and Tenfelde 1992).

system, which was introduced in Germany for the first time in Strasbourg in 1907, before spreading to another 13 cities by 1913 (Deutsche Gesellschaft zur Bekämpfung der Arbeitslosigkeit 1913).

These measures against unemployment led to the growing intervention of municipalities in the labour market and labour-management relations. The introduction of unemployment insurance could therefore be perceived as a turning point from classical liberalism based on laissez faire to social liberalism, which justified the intervention of the government not at the state but at the municipal level. To understand the background to this change in political thought in German municipalities, we have to direct our attention to 'the social task of the municipality', a dominant concept in political philosophy at the turn of the century.

By linking the various policies concerned with urban problems under this philosophy, municipal officials aimed to realise the '*Gemeinwohl*' (public welfare) of all the inhabitants in the city, especially by improving the standard of living of the lower classes. The intervention of a municipality was justified as necessary to carry out this 'task', although self-help and non-intervention in the market were still regarded as basic principles. The shaping of the 'task' was fostered by the growing influence of the Social Democratic Party in many councils from the end of the nineteenth century as a result of the increasing number of labourers who possessed suffrage. In this context, the liberal bourgeoisie hoped that adopting 'the social task of the municipality' as their platform would enable them to overcome class conflict and integrate urban society. The measures taken to tackle the unemployment problem were considered to be vital to the accomplishment of this 'task' (Mori 2009a, b). Therefore, examination of communal unemployment insurance systems may contribute not only to our understanding of the evolution of municipal social policy but also provide insights into the process by which classical liberalism was replaced by social liberalism.

However, the tendency of historical studies of German social policy has been to view communal unemployment insurance as nothing more than an unsuccessful precursor of the state system. Karl-Christian Führer, Anselm Faust and Naoki Fukuzawa, for example, saw the Genter system as a miserable mechanism that could never succeed since non-organised labourers were excluded even though they faced the highest risks of unemployment and the greatest difficulties in organising self-help (Faust 1986; Führer 1990; Fukuzawa 2007). However, they did not clarify the historical context of the Genter system, which is important from the point of view of urban history. This point has only been deeply analysed in an article by Henning, while Wolfgang Hofmann, Wolfgang R. Krabbe and Keiichi Kitazumi have undertaken institutional overviews of the Genter System (Hofmann 1984; Krabbe 1981; Kitazumi 1990). Henning showed that the Genter system spread mainly in southern Germany and was not introduced in any municipality in industrialized Rhein-Westfalen and Saxony, pointing out that it was difficult to introduce it into industrial cities because their policies were strongly influenced by big companies. However, he did not refer to controversies about introducing the Genter system in these municipalities, and hence could not shed light on how this process reflected changes in political thought (Henning 1974).

The limitations and problems of the Genter system were recognized by municipal officials of those times. At the third general meeting of the Deutscher Städtetag (Association of German Cities) held in 1911, the majority of the members agreed that the Genter system should not continue because of its limitations, and that unemployment insurance should be managed not by individual municipalities but by the Reich. Thus, the meeting decided that the Städtetag should present the Bundesrat (the Upper House) with a petition for introducing unemployment insurance at the level of the Reich that would make the insurance of seasonal labourers obligatory. At this meeting, Franz Adickes, the mayor of Frankfurt am Main and a prime advocate of 'the social task of the municipality', was at the forefront of the critics of the Genter system. He opposed not only the Genter system but also the inclusion of unemployment insurance itself in 'the social task of the municipality' (Deutscher Städtetag 1911; Mori 2011).

This begs the question, however, of why the Genter system was accepted by some municipalities despite strong opposition from municipal officials. We examine this point by focusing on 'the social task of municipalities', using a case study of municipalities in the Greater Berlin[2] administration union, especially Schöneberg and Charlottenburg. They considered the introduction of the Genter system, with some modifications, in the period around 1910, when there was general recognition that it had both strong and weak aspects. In the following analysis, we use primary sources owned by Landesarchiv Berlin and Senatsbibliothek Berlin.

2 Differences of Opinion Regarding Unemployment Insurance Among Municipalities in Greater Berlin

It was in the winter of 1907/1908, a period of serious depression, when unemployment insurance first became a political issue in the municipalities of Greater Berlin. The municipalities of Schöneberg and Charlottenburg were the most positive about introducing it and collected both domestic and foreign evidence, such as statistics and guidelines. In Charlottenburg, Ignanz Jastrow, economist and member of the Magistrat (municipal administration), led the investigation and published a memorandum that attracted the attention of other specialists and became a guideline for German municipalities at that time. Even today, it is seen as an important source of historical perspective on this topic (Jastrow and Badtke 1910; Stadtverordneten-Versammlung zu Schöneberg 1909).

[2] The Greater Berlin administration union consisted of the city of Berlin and its seven neighbouring cities, 59 rural communities and 26 Gutsbezirke (manorial districts). It was founded on April 1, 1912, to deal with matters that each municipality could not address alone, such as the tram network, city planning and the management of forests, parks and ponds. As the name 'Greater Berlin' was used to refer to this area before the shaping of an administration union, we will use 'Greater Berlin' for the area when referring to it in the period before April 1912 (Erbe 2002).

In contrast with these two municipalities, the municipality of Berlin took a negative attitude. Although a committee for this issue comprising members of the Magistrat and the city council was established in Berlin in January 1908, no meeting was held in the first half of the year because the Magistrat refused to send any members. The Social Democratic Party representatives on the city council repeatedly asked the Magistrat to hold a meeting, and this finally happened in September 1908 (Source 1). Owing to the negative attitude of the Magistrat, the committee was unable to prepare a bill to introduce unemployment insurance, but it succeeded in holding a meeting of the municipalities in Greater Berlin for an exchange of opinions on the matter (Source 2).

At this meeting, which was held in January 1910 and involved delegations from seven municipalities and two districts, the opinions of Berlin stood in contrast with those of Schöneberg and Charlottenburg. The delegation from Berlin pointed out that the exclusion of non-organized labourers was a serious weakness of the Genter system, and maintained that the municipalities should have the right to obligate them to be included. It also said that if Schöneberg and Charlottenburg introduced their own insurance systems, it would prevent the municipalities from establishing an integrated system for the whole Greater Berlin area. This meant, therefore, that depending on the decision of the third general meeting of the Deutscher Städtetag, which had already been scheduled, the municipalities should appeal to the Reich to grant them the right to establish a compulsory insurance system. Until then, they should take a wait-and-see policy (Source 3, pp. 2, 10).

In contrast, the delegations of Schöneberg and Charlottenburg saw communal systems based on the Genter system as the only realistic way to deal with the unemployment problem, given that a nationwide system could not be expected. They believed that it would take a long time to realize compulsory insurance through the process proposed by Berlin, although a legal framework that included non-organized labourer was certainly desirable. Hence, they concluded that the municipalities that had already begun to plan their own systems did not need to wait (Source 3, pp. 5–7).

Meanwhile, the eastern and northern municipalities and districts with a large number of labourers, such as Rixdorf, Boxhagen-Rummelsburg and Niederbarnimm, complained of being unable to establish their own systems, since, unlike the wealthy municipalities of Schöneberg and Charlottenburg, they suffered from a lack of resources. Furthermore, in the case of Rixdorf, there was no trade union to provide out-of-work members with unemployment benefits. Given this background, they desired an integrated system for the whole of Greater Berlin with costs shared by all municipalities in proportion to their population (Source 3, pp. 8, 12, 14).

This meeting shows that by 1910 unemployment insurance was regarded as a common issue for the municipalities of Greater Berlin. It is also clear that the municipalities had reached agreement on taking some measures to deal with the unemployment problem, given the lack of a national system, despite differences of opinion about how the measures should be organized. Schöneberg and Charlottenburg sought their own system, while the majority of the others looked for a regional system as had been proposed by Berlin.

3 The Argument for Communal Unemployment Insurance: Schöneberg and Charlottenburg

Schöneberg and Charlottenburg were originally rural communities belonging to the district of Teltow. The former was located in the southwest of Berlin, and the latter in the west. As Table 3.1 shows, from the 1870s, the population of both communities grew faster than that of Greater Berlin as a whole. Thus, the two cities came to be administered as districts in their own right, Charlottenburg in 1877, and Schöneberg 40 years later (Schütte 1988; Viergutz 1988).

In Schöneberg in 1907, secondary industry accounted for 38.5% of the total labour force and tertiary for 29.4%. The former sector consisted mainly of construction, clothing, machine manufacturing and food. Small companies dominated both sectors: there were only 10 companies with more than 200 employees among a total of 9,301, while those with fewer than five employees accounted for more than 90% of the total. On the other hand, the social structure of Schöneberg was characterized by a relatively large share of wealthy people, such as civil and military officers, pensioners and those making a living through their own property, In fact, among all Prussian municipalities with more than 5,000 people, it had the highest share of citizens liable for income tax, and came fifth in terms of total tax revenue per capita (Magistrat der Stadt Schöneberg 1910).

In Charlottenburg, the industrialization that began in the 1880s was led by the electric industry and machine construction. In contrast to Schöneberg, there were many large companies: for example, in 1907, 132 companies employed more than 51 people, and 27 companies more than 200. The growth of industrialization increased the number of fabric labourers in the city, so that in 1907 the number in the category 'fabric labourer, officer of lower rank and servant', stood at 117,000. About 20,000 people were categorized as 'without occupation', but more than 65% of them were wealthy people such as pensioners and those making a living through their own property. This was only natural since from the mid-nineteenth century Charlottenburg had been developed as 'garden city' for wealthy Berliners. Hence,

Table 3.1 The population of Greater Berlin (1871–1905)

	1871	1885	1895	1905
Berlin	826,000	1,315,000	1,677,000	2,040,000
Charlottenburg	19,587	42,371	132,377	239,559
Lichtenberg	4,754	21,976	46,741	88,380
Rixdorf (renamed Neukölln in 1912)	8,125	22,775	59,945	153,513
Schöneberg	4,555	15,872	62,695	141,010
Spandau	20,451	32,507	55,841	70,295
Steglitz	1,899	8,501	16,528	32,825
Wilmersdorf	1,662	3,616	14,351	63,568
Total of Greater Berlin	915,000	1,537,000	2,218,000	3,131,000

Source: Erbe (2002), p. 694

in 1905 Charlottenburg was ranked third in terms of total income tax revenue among all Prussian municipalities, being exceeded only by Berlin and Frankfurt am Main (Escher 1980; Schütte 1988).

These profiles show that an abundance of financial resources was the common factor behind the positive view taken by both cities regarding unemployment insurance. The Magistrats of both municipalities had presented their arguments for introducing independent systems to their city councils before they embarked on concrete plans. In the case of Charlottenburg the proposals were based on the above-mentioned memorandum by Jastrow; in Schöneberg a similar memorandum was presented by Hermann Leidig (a member of the Magistrat)

First, to justify introducing unemployment insurance, Jastrow and Leidig mentioned the term 'involuntary unemployment' (*unverschuldete Arbeitslosigkeit*). They suggested that this would occur as a result of the growing tendency of the Reich to intervene in the market through the introduction of protective tariffs and also because of the monopolization of the market through the growth of big companies and cartels. Involuntary unemployment referred to a situation where workers were unable to find suitable jobs, despite being able and willing to work (Jastrow and Badtke 1910; Leidig 1911). This concept came to the fore as a result of what had happened during the depression of the 1870s to the 1890s and also due to the development of the trade cycle theory. This led people to recognise that unemployment was not the fault of individual workers, but a social phenomenon that had deeper roots (Faust 1986).

Jastrow and Leidig were therefore of the opinion that insurance should be limited to people with the ability to help themselves, such as skilled labourers and white-collar workers. Leidig also pointed out that for these groups the *Krisenarbeit* was inadequate, since their health suffered from the unaccustomed hard physical work that it required them to perform during the winter. Unemployment benefits without labour obligations would, in Leidig's opinion, be more humane treatment for those who were not accustomed to physical work. In addition, if self-help was a prerequisite, unemployment benefits would be seen as a justified demand of the unemployed, not a 'blessing', as was the case in poor relief, and hence would not wound their self-esteem. In addition, Leidig expected that by rescuing the insured from extreme difficulties – from the 'seeds of disease or immorality' – during periods of unemployment, insurance would reduce the cost of poor relief and medical care. These arguments suggest that the fundamental purpose of introducing communal unemployment insurance was to save people with the ability to help themselves from becoming paupers (Leidig 1911, pp. 15–16, 26–27).[3]

As to the second point, Jastrow and Leidig recognized that the best organization for managing unemployment insurance was the Reich, but both argued that the municipalities should pioneer the issue, because they believed that it was not feasible for the Reich to do so (Jastrow and Badtke 1910; Leidig 1911). Leidig explained

[3] Jastrow was also of the opinion that fundamentally, unemployment insurance should focus on supporting skilled labourers, although his argument was based on less concrete explanations than Leidig's (Jastrow and Badtke 1910).

the reason in more detail. He expected that if a municipality launched an unemployment insurance plan on its own initiative, workers with high unemployment risk might migrate to the city. Yet despite the fear that they would be 'pulling chestnuts out of the fire', the municipalities should, Leidig said, introduce the Genter system, not only because it was the municipalities' responsibility to save their inhabitants from becoming paupers, but because of the expectation that the spread of the Genter system would, owing to its political attributes, provoke the Reich to establish insurance at the national level (Leidig 1911, pp. 20–23).

The political attributes of the Genter system were related to the third point of Jastrow's and Leidig's arguments, which involved the merits of the system. They both supported the Genter system because it called for union dues to fund unemployment benefits, therefore encouraging workers to rely on self-help, as well as because using the existing framework of trade union unemployment benefits would make it easier to set up the communal system. Another advantage was that depending on the trade unions to give unemployment benefits would make it possible to avoid the misuse of benefits, since the unions were in the best situation to grasp the actual conditions of the unemployed (Jastrow and Badtke 1910; Leidig 1911).

In spite of these merits, however, most municipal officials saw the Genter system as a form of financial support for the trade unions which, by allowing them to increase their strike funds, would encourage the labour movement, and eventually strengthen the influence of the Social Democratic Party. That was the view of opponents such as Franz Adickes, who was mentioned above (Faust 1986; Henning 1974). By contrast, Jastrow was of the opinion that by giving trade unions responsibility for paying unemployment benefits, the Genter system would enable the municipality to keep the labour movement under control. According to Jastrow, the development of social insurance from the 1880s had weakened the presence of the trade unions by taking away their role as providers of relief. Hence, he concluded that if the Reich deprived the trade unions of their unemployment benefits, strikes would become the only way for them to make an impact and the labour movement would be strengthened (Jastrow and Badtke 1910). This argument was related to the fact that since the 1890s, the Free Trade Union had fallen under the influence of revisionism and tended to avoid strikes (Schönhoven 1980).

4 The Development of the Schöneberger System

Early communal unemployment insurance in Germany was based solely on the Genter system, as in the case of Strasbourg. However, since the exclusion of non-organized labourers was seen as a serious flaw, municipalities such as Schöneberg and Charlottenburg attempted to supplement it by introducing sub-systems (Deutsche Gesellschaft zur Bekämpfung der Arbeitslosigkeit 1913). As Table 3.2 shows, the Schöneberger system combined the Genter system with the Spar and lunch supply systems, both of which were aimed at non-organized labourers, in order to include all labourers and white-collar workers who had been living in the

Table 3.2 Outline of the Schöneberger System

	Genter system	Spar system	Lunch supply system
Prerequisite	Residence in the city for more than 1 year and "involuntary unemployment"		
Insured	Members of trade unions that provided their out-of-work members with unemployment benefits	Non-organized labourers who had been depositing money in the sparkasse	Non-organized labourers who had no account in the Sparkasse
Uncovered cases	Strikes and lockouts		
Standards of benefits	The municipality subsidised the unemployment benefits of trade unions by 50% (maximum of 1 Mark per day)	The municipality subsidised withdrawals from the Sparkasse by 50% (maximum of 1 Mark per day)	The municipality gave meal coupons to the unemployed and their families from October 1. to March 31. (maximum of 0.60 Marks per day for a family)
Period of benefits	A maximum of 60 days per year		
Termination of benefits	Reemployment or refusal to accept a job arranged by the municipal employment office		
Waiting period	Three weeks after the day of the application to the trade union	One week after the day of the application to the communal employment office	
Obligation	The unemployed had to go to the communal employment office every day while they were receiving the benefits in order to look for a job		

Source: Leidig (1911), pp. 40–47

city for more than 1 year. The Spar system was aimed at non-organized labourers who had been depositing money in the Sparkasse (the municipal saving bank) as an alternative to the Genter system, by making the standard and period of benefits in the former system the same as in the latter. The lunch supply system was aimed at those who could not save any money, to provide them with meals at communal kitchens managed by private charities in winter, when unemployment was the most severe.

The main purpose of combining the three systems was to foster the spirit of self-help in labourers and white-collar workers, through introducing the Genter system for organized labourers and the Spar system for those who were not organized. The reason for establishing identical standards and periods of benefits for both systems was, on the one hand, to treat both organized and non-organized labourers equally, and on the other hand, to weaken the labour movement by reducing the attraction of the unemployment benefits provided by trade unions. In contrast with these two systems, the lunch supply system was not contributory, so it could not foster self-help directly. Leidig expected, however, that the lunch supply system could also make an indirect contribution to self-help since labourers and white-collar workers with relatively large incomes had such an aversion to communal kitchens that they would be encouraged to join the Spar system (Leidig 1911).

At a city council meeting on November 10, 1910, the Magistrat proposed the introduction of the Schöneberger system as a substitute for the *Krisenarbeit*, and its annual budget of 15,000 Marks. The proposition won the approval of all parties, especially because of the inclusion of non-organized labourers, although there were criticisms of the fact that more than one year's residence had been made a prerequisite (Stadtverordneten-Versammlung zu Schöneberg 1910; Schöneberger Tageblatt 1910). The Schöneberger system operated from January 26, 1911 to October 12, 1914, when *Allgemeine Erwerbslosenfüsorge* (general unemployment relief) was introduced as a wartime welfare measure (Städtisches Arbeitsamt Berlin-Schöneberg 1916/1919).

Table 3.3 shows that the total number of recipients of unemployment benefit increased from 502 in 1911 to 1,040 in 1914, with more than 80% of all applications accepted each year. Of the three sub-systems, the Genter system had the highest degree of uptake. Even so, its shares in three categories (number of recipients, total number of days and total amount of benefits) began to fall from 1911 to 1913, while the share of the Spar system increased rapidly. It should also be noted that during the same period, the amount of benefits per capita given by the Spar system showed a consistent excess of about 5 Marks over the Genter system, while the total number of days was almost the same in both systems. This suggests that it was non-organized labourers with relatively high incomes who enrolled in the Spar system. Table 3.4 shows that more than 90% of those insured by the Genter system belonged to the Free Trade Union, especially to organizations for skilled labourers, such as metalworkers, printers and carpenters (Städtisches Arbeitsamt Berlin-Schöneberg 1913).

Therefore, we can assume that the Schöneberger system achieved its expected aim in supporting organized skilled labourers through the Genter system, while the effect of the Spar system, which was designed for non-organized labourers who were able to pay for insurance, was more limited. The labour bureau of the municipality attributed this to the residency requirement, as most unskilled labourers, who formed the majority of non-organized labourers, changed residence frequently (Kommunale Praxis 1911). This point was proved by the fact that the lunch supply system accounted for a very small share in the number of recipients (2.2–3.6%), as is shown by Table 3.3.

5 The Failure of the Attempt to Introduce the Charlottenburger System

As Table 3.5 shows, the Magistrat of Charlottenburg devised its own system, the Charlottenburger system, by uniting the municipal system and the Spar system with the Genter system. The contents of both the latter sub-systems were similar to those in the Schöneberger system, while the municipal system was a form of voluntary

Table 3.3 The development of the Schöneberger System

1. Numbers of unemployment benefit recipients

Year	Genter system		Spar system		Lunch supply system		Total (a)	Applicants (b)	(a)/(b)
1911	479	95.4%	8	1.6%	15	3.0%	502	600	83.7%
1912	620	91.9%	40	5.9%	15	2.2%	675	768	87.9%
1913	711	84.7%	98	11.7%	30	3.6%	839	982	85.4%
1914	930	89.4%	82	7.9%	28	2.7%	1,040	1,205	86.3%

2. Period of benefits (in days)

Year	Genter system			Spar system			Lunch supply system			Total
	Total number of days		Per capita	Total number of days		Per capita	Total number of days		Per capita	
1911	10,908	96.7%	23	192	1.7%	24	183	1.6%	12	11,283
1912	15,570	91.9%	25	987	5.8%	25	177	1.0%	12	16,934
1913	21,318	85.9%	30	2,950	11.9%	30	488	2.0%	16	24,816
1914	22,925	90.8%	25	1,823	7.2%	22	444	1.8%	16	25,239

3. Amount of benefits (in Marks)

Year	Genter system			Spar system			Lunch supply system			Total
	Amount of benefits		Per capita	Amount of benefits		Per capita	Amount of benefits		Per capita	
1911	8,749.00	96.9%	18.27	192.00	2.1%	24.00	90.30	1.0%	6.02	9,031.30
1912	12,631.00	92.1%	20.37	987.00	7.2%	24.68	100.20	0.7%	6.68	13,718.20
1913	17,478.36	84.3%	24.58	2,946.57	14.2%	30.07	317.60	1.5%	10.59	20,742.53
1914	17,692.74	88.9%	19.02	1,819.83	9.1%	22.19	385.10	1.9%	13.75	19,897.67

Sources: Geschäftsbericht des städtischen Arbeitsamts Berlin-Schöneberg 1913, pp. 5–6; 1914/1915, pp. 7–8; Kommunale Praxis, Jg. 13, Nr. 36 (6. September 1913), Sp. 1127ff

Note: The year 1911 = from January 26, 1911 to December 1911; the year 1914 = from January 1, 1914 to October 12, 1914; the other years = from January 1 to December 31

Table 3.4 Results of the Genter system as part of the Schöneberger System in 1913

Name of trade unions	Number of unemployment benefit recipients	Period of the benefits (in total days)	Amount of benefits (in Marks)
Free trade union	654 (92.0%)	19,635 (92.1%)	16,332.18 (93.4%)
Hirsch-Duncker union	6 (0.8%)	139 (0.7%)	132.88 (0.8%)
Christian trade union	6 (0.8%)	110 (0.5%)	71.64 (0.4%)
Other trade unions	45 (6.3%)	1434 (6.7%)	941.66 (5.4%)
Total	705 (100.0%)	21,208 (100.0%)	17,406.72 (100.0%)

Source: Geschäftsbericht des städtischen Arbeitsamts Berlin-Schöneberg 1913, pp. 13–14

Table 3.5 Outline of the Charlottenburger System

	Genter system	Spar system	Municipal system
Prerequisite	Residence in the city for more than 1 year		Residence in the city for more than 6 months and employment for more than 48 weeks per year in the last 2 years
Insured	Members of trade unions that provided their out-of-work members with unemployment benefits	Nonorganized laborers who had deposited more than 30 Marks in the Sparkasse over the last 12 months	Residence in the city for more than 6 months and employment for more than 48 weeks per year in the last 2 years
Uncovered cases	Strikes and lockouts, disease, accidents, invalid, pregnancy and childbirth		
Standards of benefits	The municipality subsidised the unemployment benefits of trade unions by 50% (maximum of 1 Mark per day	The municipality subsidised withdrawals from the Sparkasse by 50% (maximum of 1 Mark per day)	Benefits amounted to 1 Mark per day
Period of benefits	A maximum of 60 days per year		
Termination of benefits	Re-employment or refusal to accept a job arranged by the communal employment office		
Waiting period	One week		

Source: Vorlagen für die Stadtverordneten-Versammlung zu Charlottenburg 1911, pp. 136–140

insurance managed by the municipality. The municipal system was expected to function as an additional group insurance for members of trade unions with their own system for unemployment benefits as well as support for non-organized labourers. There was no difference in the contents of the additional group system insurance and the individual system. The total annual budget of the municipality for the Charlottenburger system was estimated at 10,000 Marks. In the first year, the municipality would also have to invest 20,000 Marks together with contributions from private charities and employers in order to provide the funds needed for the municipal system. After that its annual costs were to come from the contributions of those who were insured, private charities and employers, as well as from an annual municipal budget of 3,000 Marks (Stadtverordnetenversammlung zu Charlottenburg 1911).

At a meeting of the city council on May 22, 1912, the Magistrat proposed the introduction of the Charlottenburger system, but the Liberal Party made strong objections. The main reason for their opposition came from the fact that most of the beneficiaries of the Schöneberger system belonged to the Free Trade Union. In order to weaken the influence of the Social Democratic Party they considered that the municipality should abandon the idea of introducing the Genter system, proposing that the Charlottenburger System should be based only on the municipal system. The Magistrat offered a counter-argument that the Genter system was the only realistic way to foster the spirit of self-help among labourers, given that unemployment insurance at the national level could not be expected. The Magistrat warned that if the municipality introduced the municipal system alone, labourers who faced a high risk of unemployment would be encouraged to migrate to the city. This argument was supported by the Social Democratic Party. In their view, the primary intention behind the opposition to the Genter System was the desire to ensure that labourers would be dependent on company-based welfare. On the other hand, the Social Democratic Party opposed the municipal system, saying that it would 'harm the trade unions by pushing them aside'. It suggested that the municipality, trade unions and employers were competing against each other for hegemony over unemployment insurance. In the end, the proposition of the Magistrat was rejected owing to the opposition of the Liberal Party, although some of their members considered the Genter system to be the most realistic because 'promoting the labourer's welfare [by introducing it] would be in the interest of the municipality', despite its 'side effects' (Magistrat der Stadt Charlottenburg. 1912, pp. 216–223).

As a result, the Magistrat designed a new system, based on a revised version of the municipal system, with an annual municipal budget of 10,000 Marks. There were remarkable differences between the old and revised municipal systems with respect to the rules about benefits and the contributions of the insured: the benefits for individual insurance were raised from 1.00 Mark per day to 1.50 Marks, while the benefits for group insurance were reduced to 0.75 Marks. The contributions for individual insurance were left unchanged at 0.25 Marks per week, while contributions for group insurance were reduced to 0.10 Marks (Stadtverordnetenversammlung zu Charlottenburg 1912). These changes showed that the Magistrat intended to increase the number of non-organized labourers who were insured by raising their benefits, and to substitute the revised system for the Genter system by making it easier for organized labourers to join.

The revised municipal system was proposed at a city council meeting on December 4, 1912 but it met with strong opposition from both the Social Democratic and Liberal Parties. The former objected not only to the omission of the Genter system, but also to the fact that employment for more than 48 weeks per year in the past 2 years had been introduced as a prerequisite. This was because those who could satisfy such a prerequisite were unlikely to require unemployment insurance in the first place. Hence, they argued that the proposed system was 'called unemployment insurance; however, [it] could not function as such in reality'. Besides, they pointed out, introducing the new system would make it difficult for municipalities in the Greater Berlin area to keep in step with each other, given that another system had already been put in place in Schöneberg. Based on these reasons, the Social Democratic Party called for the wholesale abandonment of the scheme. By contrast, the Liberal Party criticized the proposal to reduce the contribution of organized labourers. This, they said, would strengthen the position of the Free Trade Union just like the Genter system, since group insurance would be managed not by the municipality directly, but by trade unions or employers. If group insurance was not omitted from the system, they also argued that unemployment insurance itself should be abandoned. For its part, the Magistrat seemed to persist with the idea that communal unemployment insurance would only function well if the city adopted the original Charlottenburger system by integrating the Genter and municipal systems. Therefore, it was reluctant to continue talks with the two Parties with a view to the introduction of the revised municipal system. The Magistrat did argue, however, that the new system could play an important role in encouraging the Reich to come up with its own unemployment insurance, although a communal system without the Genter system could not be expected to achieve much (Magistrat der Stadt Charlottenburg 1912, pp. 437–447).

The conclusion was postponed until a final reading held on December 17, 1912. At the start of this session, the Social Democratic Party proposed a motion that had the following three points: (1) increasing the annual budget of the municipality from 10,000 to 100,000 Marks; (2) dropping the prerequisite of employment for more than 48 weeks per year in the past 2 years and (3) limiting group insurance to members of trade unions. According to them, if this motion was not accepted, the municipal system would be 'doomed to failure' and communal unemployment insurance itself should therefore be abandoned. Those members of the Liberal Party who hoped to establish communal unemployment insurance in any form saw the motion of the Social Democratic Party as a 'demonstration' intended to conceal their desire to encourage rejection of the Magistrat's proposition. However, as the third point of the motion would bring the Municipal System closer to the Genter system, this 'demonstration' stiffened the attitude of the majority in the Liberal Party. It was not the Magistrat but a minority of the Liberal Party who exerted themselves to gain agreement for the revised municipal system, in opposition to the majority of their Party and to the Social Democratic Party. They argued that accepting the Magistrat's proposition would give the city an opportunity to develop a better system in the future. Despite their support, the Magistrat's proposition was rejected by the city council and the attempt to introduce communal unemployment insurance in Charlottenburg ended in failure (Magistrat der Stadt Charlottenburg 1912, pp. 468–483).

6 The Failure of the Attempt to Introduce Unemployment Insurance for the Whole of the Greater Berlin Area

The struggles of the Schöneberg and Charlottenburg Magistrats led other municipalities to plan their own strategies. For example, in July 1913 the Magistrat of Neukölln (former Rixdorf)[4] proposed that the Greater Berlin administration union should introduce unemployment insurance for the whole area. He viewed the fact that insurance existed only in Schöneberg as problematic, since two factors would cause conflicts between municipalities, if each municipality, following Schöneberg, introduced its own system. The first factor was that labourers did not necessarily work in the place where they lived. For example, 46.4% of the labourers who lived in Neukölln were employed in other municipalities of Greater Berlin. This meant that if each municipality insured its own inhabitants, serious imbalances would arise in the financial burden that different municipalities would have to carry. The residency prerequisite was the second factor. Although it was needed to prevent labourers with a high risk of unemployment from flowing into those municipalities that offered insurance, it would make the insuring of non-organized labourers with high mobility issues difficult, as was clear from the case of Schöneberg. The Magistrat of Neukölln argued that both problems would be solved if the Greater Berlin administration union established unemployment insurance for the whole area. He recommended the original Charlottenburger system as the most feasible scheme, even though it had not been adopted (Source 4).

In September 1913, a meeting of the administration union of Greater Berlin was held to discuss the proposition of the Magistrat of Neukölln. At this meeting, his supporters voiced their concern that the Reich would leave the responsibility for introducing unemployment insurance to individual municipalities. Their anxiety arose from the fact that the Reich had done nothing even though the Deutscher Städtetag had presented the Bundesrat with a petition for the introduction of unemployment insurance throughout the country in September 1911 (Source 5).

As the participation of Berlin was indispensable to the implementation of an insurance scheme for the whole of Greater Berlin, the Magistrats of some municipalities, including Lichtenberg and Schöneberg, had already asked the Magistrat of Berlin to take the initiative. The Magistrat of Berlin was, however, against the proposition of Neukölln for the following reasons. First, the Genter system, which was the basis of the Charlottenburger system, excluded non-organized labourers. The Spar and municipal systems were also likely to exclude them if they were designed as voluntary forms of insurance. Second, if the administration union of Greater Berlin introduced a system that made the insurance of non-organized labourers compulsory, numerous labourers with a high risk of unemployment would emigrate from other regions into Greater Berlin. Finally, in order to avoid such a problem, it was necessary for the Reich to introduce an insurance scheme covering the whole of Germany (Source 5).

[4] In 1912, the city of Rixdorf changed its name to Neukölln (Cf. Erbe 2002).

The argument of Berlin was supported by many municipalities, including Charlottenburg, Spandau and Friedenau. For example, Alexander Dominicus, the mayor of Schöneberg, agreed that a nationwide insurance scheme would be effective in including non-organized labourers, through pointing to the results of the Schöneberger system (Source 5). Thus, the meeting concluded that the administration union of Greater Berlin should present the Reichskanzler (Imperial Chancellor) with a petition for the introduction of a nationwide unemployment insurance system that would include compulsory insurance for the non-organized labourers of industrial sectors such as the construction industry (Source 6). This decision was similar to that taken by the third general meeting of the Deutscher Städtetag in 1911. It therefore signals an end to attempts to introduce unemployment insurance at the level of Greater Berlin. Even after the petition had been presented to the Reichskanzler, the Social Democratic Party in Berlin continued to press for the introduction of the Genter system, but it was unable to override the Magistrat's decision.[5] The stand taken by Berlin determined the attitudes of the other municipalities in Greater Berlin, so that Schöneberg was the only municipality in the region that had introduced unemployment insurance before World War I.

7 Conclusion

In Greater Berlin, the majority of municipalities took a cautious attitude to the introduction of unemployment insurance, although they considered that since the Reich was unlikely to do anything it was necessary for individual municipalities themselves to take some sort of action. The proactive attitudes of Schöneberg and Charlottenburg reflected this viewpoint and encouraged other municipalities to plan their own strategies. One result was the Magistrat of Neukölln's proposal for an unemployment insurance scheme for the whole of Greater Berlin. Schöneberg and Charlottenburg took the lead because they had greater financial resources than the other municipalities. Even so, the amounts that they proposed to spend, estimated at 15,000 and 10,000 Marks respectively, were a minute portion of their total revenues, which amounted to 21.11 million and 40.97 million Marks in 1908 (Silbergleit 1908). This shows that the issue in both municipalities was not the financial burden that unemployment insurance would cause, but the justification of public intervention that it would provide.

In this context, Leidig made an important point when he stated that the spread of the Genter system would put political pressure on the Reich to establish an insurance system at the national level. This political aspect of the Genter system was also

[5] The Social Democratic Party in Berlin later gave up its push to introduce unemployment insurance, but in the winter 1913/1914 demanded the establishment of a 500,000 Marks provisional relief fund for the unemployed. Residence in the city for more than one year was to be the only prerequisite with the maximum payment being 1 Mark per day. This proposition also failed owing to the opposition of the Magistrat (Cf. Source 7; Source 8; Source 9).

a crucial point in the controversies that it provoked. For example, Jastrow argued that keeping the trade unions as organizations for mutual relief through the Genter system would enable Charlottenburg to keep the labour movement under control. This logic was also used by municipal officials who supported the introduction of the Genter system at the third general meeting of the Deutscher Städtetag in 1911. Thus, we can assume that Jastrow's opinion greatly influenced arguments in favour of the system. In addition, the Social Democratic Party in Charlottenburg had always taken precautions to ensure that the Magistrat did not use insurance as a way of weakening trade unions and eventually opposed the introduction of insurance for this reason. This case proved Jastrow right. From the cases of Schöneberg and Charlottenburg, we can find agreement among the advocates and opponents of the Genter system on ways to weaken the labour movement, despite their completely contrasting views of the system.

Moreover, the reason why the Schöneberger and Charlottenburger systems were based on the Genter System can be found in the essential aim of unemployment insurance, which was to prevent people with self-help abilities, such as skilled labourers, from becoming paupers. In both systems, there were attempts to include non-organized labourers as far as possible through the establishment of sub-systems such as the Spar and municipal systems, but since the main purpose of the sub-systems was the indirect fostering of self-help, there was no compulsory element.

From these findings, it can be seen that unemployment insurance was justified as a way of fulfilling 'the social task of the municipality', as it was seen as public intervention to overcome class conflict and integrate urban society. Besides, the fact that the Genter system was aimed at fostering collective self-help by paying subsidies to the trade unions shows the similarity between unemployment insurance and other policies in the category of 'the social task of the municipality'. In housing policy, for example, the construction of municipal housing for those on low incomes was regarded as less important than indirect support for cooperative associations for the construction of housing, by guaranteeing loans, reducing taxation, introducing charges for street building and so on. As members of the cooperative association made joint investments in constructing their own houses, we could also consider this as collective self-help (Kitamura 2007; Lees and Lees 2007; Mori 2009a). Hence, the common feature of the practice of 'the social task of the municipality' can be found in public intervention to foster collective self-help. This point shows a clear difference between communal unemployment insurance based on the Genter system and the national one introduced by the Reich in 1927, since the latter made insurance compulsory for all labourers in Germany. Viewed from this perspective, we can derive the conclusion that the logic of 'the social task of the municipality' contributed to the establishment of communal unemployment insurance in Wilhelminian Germany, but also had its imperfections, since there were limitations on those who could be insured.

Acknowledgments The author is grateful to JSPS KAKENHI (Grant Number JP 22730279) for financial support for the research and to the Hitotsubashi University for financial support for the first copy editing of this paper by a native English speaker.

References

Deutsche Gesellschaft zur Bekämpfung der Arbeitslosigkeit. 1913. *Der gegenwärtige Stand der Arbeitslosenfürsorge und -versicherung in Deutschland. Eine Erhebung der Deutschen Gesellschaft zur Bekämpfung der Arbeitslosigkeit.* Berlin: Heymann.

Deutscher Städtetag. 1911. *Verhandlungen des dritten Deutschen Städtetages am 11. und 12. September 1911 zu Posen.* Berlin: W. & D. Loewenthal.

Erbe, Michael. 2002. Berlin im Kaiserreich (1871–1918). In *Geschichte Berlins. Bd. 2. Von der Märzrevolution bis zur Gegenwart*, 3. erweiterte und aktualisierte Auflage, ed. Wolfgang Ribbe. Berlin: Berliner Wissenschafts-Verlag.

Escher, Felix. 1980. Die Westausdehnung Charlottenburgs 1900–1945. In *Von der Residenz zur City. 275 Jahre Charlottenburg*, ed. Wolfgang Ribbe. Berlin: Colloquium-Verlag.

Faust, Anselm. 1986. *Arbeitsmarktpolitik im Deutschen Kaiserreich: Arbeitsvermittlung, Arbeitsbeschaffung und Arbeitslosenversicherung 1890–1918.* Stuttgart: F. Steiner.

Führer, Karl-Christian. 1990. *Arbeitslosigkeit und die Entstehung der Arbeitslosenversicherung in Deutschland 1902–1927.* Berlin: Colloquium Verlag.

Fukuzawa, Naoki. 2007. Doitsu ni okeru shakaikokka no michi: Daini teiseiki kara gendai ni itaru made no rekishiteki keiken [The Path to the 'Sozialstaat' (Social State) in Germany: Historical Experience in Germany from the Wilhelmine Era to the Present Day]. *Rekishi to Keizai* [The Journal of Political Economy and Economic History] 195.

Henning, Hansjoachim. 1974. Arbeitslosenversicherung vor 1914: Das Genter System und seine Übernahme in Deutschland. In *Wirtschaftspolitik und Arbeitsmarkt. Bericht über die 4. Arbeitstagung der Gesellschaft für Sozial- und Wirtschaftsgeschichte in Wien am 14. und 15. April 1971*, ed. Hermann Kellenbenz. Wien: R. Oldenbourg.

Hofmann, Wolfgang. 1984. Aufgaben und Struktur der kommunalen Selbstverwaltung in der Zeit der Hochindustrialisierung. In *Deutsche Verwaltungsgeschichte. Das Deutsche Reich bis zum Ende der Monarchie*, ed. Kurt G. A. Jeserich et al. Stuttgart: Deutsche Verlags-Anstalt.

Jastrow, Ignaz, and Walter Badtke. 1910. *Kommunale Arbeitslosenversicherung. Denkschrift und Materialsammlung vorgelegt dem Magistrat Charlottenburg.* Berlin: G. Reimer.

Kitamura, Masafumi. 2007. *Doitsu jūtaku kaikaku undō: 19-seiki no toshika to shimin shakai* [The Housing Reform Movement in Germany: Urbanisation and Civil Society in the 19th Century]. Kyoto: Kyoto Daigaku Gakujutsu Shuppankai.

Kitazumi, Keiichi. 1990. *Kindai Doitsu kanryō kokka to jichi: Shakai kokka e no michi* [Germany as a Modern Bureaucratic State: Towards a Social State]. Tokyo: Seibundo.

Kommunale Praxis: *Wochenschrift für Kommunalpolitik und Gemeindesozialismus. Berlin: B. B. P. Singer*, 1911. 11(4).

Krabbe, Wolfgang R. 1981. Die Gründung städtischer Arbeiterschutz-Anstalten in Deutschland: Arbeitsnachweis, Arbeitslosenfürsorge, Gewerbegericht und Rechtsauskunftstelle. In *Arbeiterexistenz im 19. Jahrhundert. Lebensstandard und Lebensgestaltung deutscher Arbeiter und Handwerker*, ed. Werner Conze and Ulrich Engelhardt. Stuttgart: Klett-Cotta.

Lees, Andrew, and Lynn Hollen Lees. 2007. *Cities and the Making of Modern Europe, 1750–1914.* Cambridge: Cambridge University Press.

Leidig, Hermann. 1911. *Die Arbeitslosenunterstützung der Stadt Schöneberg.* Berlin: Guttentag.

Magistrat der Stadt Charlottenburg. 1912. *Amtliche Bericht über die Verhandlung der Charlottenburuger Stadtverordneten-Versammlung in den öffentlichen Sitzungen nach Stenographischer Aufnahme.* Charlottenburg: A. Gertz.

Magistrat der Stadt Schöneberg. 1910. *Verwaltungsbericht des Magistrats der Stadt Schöneberg, Bd. 3.* Berlin-Schöneberg: Gebhradt, Jahn & Landt.

Mori, Takahito. 2009a. Seiki tenkanki Doitsu ni okeru toshi seisaku rinen: 1903nen Doitsu toshi hakurankai wo chūshin ni [The Political Philosophy of German Municipalities at the Turn of the Century: A Case Study of the German Municipal Exposition (Dresden, 1903)]. *Seiyo shigaku* [Studies in Western History]. 232.

———. 2009b. Doitsu Shakai Seisaku Gakkai ni okeru kindai toshiron: K. Bücher no shoron wo jirei ni [Theories About the Modern City in the German Association for Social Policy: Karl Bücher and His Works on "The Economic Task of Municipality"]. *Keizaikei* [Quarterly Journal of Economics, Kanto Gakuin University] 240.

———. 2011. "Shakai toshi ni okeru shitsugyo hoken no tenkai": Daini teiseiki Doitsu wo jirei to shite [The Development of Unemployment Insurance in the "Social City": A Case Study of the Second German Empire]. *Rekihsi to Keizai* [The Journal of Political Economy and Economic History] 211.

Ritter, Gerhard A. 1989. *Der Sozialstaat: Entstehung und Entwicklung im internationalen Vergleich*. München: Oldenbourg.

Ritter, Gerhard A., and Klaus Tenfelde. 1992. *Arbeiter im Deutschen Kaiserreich 1871 bis 1914*. Bonn: J. H. W. Dietz.

Schöneberger Tageblatt: Gemeinde-Zeitung. Berlin: Lenz. Nr. 286 (December 7, 1910).

Schönhoven, Klaus. 1980. Selbsthilfe als Form von Solidarität. Das gewerkschaftliche Unterstützungswesen im Deutschen Kaiserreich bis 1914. *Archiv für Sozialgeschichte* 20.

Schütte, Dieter. 1988. *Geschichte der Berliner Verwaltungsbezirke. Bd. 1: Charlottenburg*. Berlin: Colloquium-Verlag.

Silbergleit, Heinrich, ed. 1908. *Preussens Städte. Denkschrift zum 100 jährigen Jubiläum der Städteordnung vom 19. November 1808*. Berlin: Heymann.

Source 1: Amtlicher stenographischer Bericht für die Sitzung der Stadtverordnetenversammlung vom 14. Mai 1908 u. vom 10. September 1908, in: Landesarchiv Berlin (LAB.), A Rep 001-02, Nr. 14.

Source 2: Amtlicher stenographischer Bericht für die Sitzung der Stadtverordnetenversammlung vom 19. Januar 1911, p. 27, in: LAB., A Rep 001-02, Nr. 14.

Source 3: Registratur der Verhandlung über die Arbeitslosenversicherung in Groß-Berlin (Berlin im Rathaus am 6. Januar 1910), pp. 2, 10, in: LAB., A Rep 001-02, Nr. 14.

Source 4: Antrag auf Einführung einer das Gebiet von Groß-Berlin umfassenden Arbeitslosenversicherung (Neukölln, den 14. Juni 1913), pp. 2–3, in: LAB., A Rep 001-02, Nr. 15.

Source 5: Abschrift des Protokolls der Besprechung vom 13. September 1913 in Sachen der Arbeitslosenversicherung, pp. 7–9, in: LAB., A Rep 001-02, Nr. 15

Source 6: Eingabe an den Herrn Reichskanzler betreffend die reichsgesetzliche Einführung der Zwangsversicherung gegen die Arbeitslosigkeit vom 18. November 1913, p. 4, in: LAB., A Rep 001-02, Nr. 15.

Source 7: Protokoll der Sitzung des Ausschusses betr. die Einrichtung einer Arbeitslosenversicherung (Berlin, 27. September 1913), in: LAB., A Rep 001-02, Nr. 16.

Source 8: Protokoll des Ausschusses zur Vorberatung des Antrages der Stadtverordneten Dr. Arons und Genossen, betreffend die Bewilligung von 500,000 M zur Unterstützung der Arbeitslosen vom 21. Januar 1914, in: LAB., A Rep 001-02, Nr. 16.

Source 9: Amtlicher stenographischer Bericht für die Sitzung der Stadtverordnetenversammlung vom 12. Januar 1914, pp. 54–55, in: LAB., A Rep 001-02, Nr. 16.

Städtisches Arbeitsamt Berlin-Schöneberg. 1913. *Geschäftsbericht des städtischen Arbeitsamts Berlin-Schöneberg*. Berlin-Schöneberg: Gebhradt, Jahn & Landt.

Stadtverordnetenversammlung zu Charlottenburg. 1911/1912. Vorlagen für die Stadtverordneten-Versammlung zu Charlottenburg. Charlottenburg.

Stadtverordneten-Versammlung zu Schöneberg. 1909/1910. Vorlagen für die Stadtverordneten-Versammlung zu Schöneberg vom 25. Januar 1909. Berlin-Schöneberg.

Viergutz, Volker. 1988. *Geschichte der Berliner Verwaltungsbezirke. Bd.5: Schöneberg*. Berlin: Colloquium-Verlag.

Chapter 4
The Short-Lived Revival of the Mechanical Engineering Industry in the Paris Region 1939–1958

Toshikatsu Nakajima

Abstract Reactivated by the drive for rearmament against Germany after 1935, the mechanical engineering industry in the Paris region survived the Vichy period (1940–1944) and post-war disturbances to blossom in the early 1950s. In the immediate post-war period, Parisian machine manufacturers profited from the absence of German firms in the global capital goods market, whereas the boom of consumer durables was just around the corner. In this sense, the 1950s was a period of transition. Before the emergence of the Common Market and the appearance in the provinces of large and fully operating assembly plants in the 1960s, small metalworking shops, traditionally located in the east end of Paris, managed to produce machines and mechanical parts in sufficient quantities and at suitable levels of quality, introducing technical innovations, specialising in particular activities and intensifying ties among themselves. After relevant statistical observations, this paper reviews company annual reports to sketch the growth of leading firms in each field of operation. It examines technological documents to clarify the practical innovations made by these small enterprises. It cites contemporary economic research in order to evaluate the capability of the production networks that appeared during the pre-war period of rearmament and show how they contributed to the post-war prosperity of French industry.

Keywords Intermediate technologies • Mechanical engineering • Paris • Post-war growth • Small firms • World War II

This chapter is a translation of an article that originally appeared in *Shakai Keizai Shigaku* 74(5) (Jan 2009), pp. 65–81.

T. Nakajima (✉)
College of Economics, Rikkyo University,
3-34-1 Nishi-ikebukuro, Toshima-ku, Tokyo 171-8501, Japan
e-mail: nakaj@rikkyo.ac.jp

S. Baba (ed.), *Economic History of Cities and Housing*, Monograph Series of the Socio-Economic History Society, Japan, DOI 10.1007/978-981-10-4097-9_4

1 Introduction

In previous works (Nakajima 1985, 1987), I have examined two periods when mechanical engineering flourished in Paris: the Second Empire, especially the 1850s, and the early twentieth century. During these periods, mechanical engineers in Paris, always referring to the tradition of luxury metalworking, promptly reorganised their systems of production and created new products, thereby contributing to European and worldwide industrial growth.

Just as these two periods corresponded chronologically to first, the formation, and then, the development, of Parisian mechanical engineering, the third period, examined here, can be construed as corresponding to the maturing of the industry. This paper clarifies how and why it prospered during the mid-twentieth century. On the one hand, from 1945 to the end of the 1950s, while West German industrialists struggled to recover from defeat, Parisian mechanical engineers were able to take their place and play an interim role in supplying Europe with industrial appliances. Meanwhile, they began transforming themselves in order to catch up with the mass-production age as consumer durables emerged in Europe. In the long run, after the 1960s, as the division of labour became worldwide even in the field of mechanical engineering, factories in and around Paris narrowly survived because of their connections with large automobile and aircraft firms. However, they had possessed many more options to attain maturity just after World War II.

The starting point of the third period of growth dates back at least to the start of rearmament in 1935. To cope with the upsurge in demand, Parisian mechanical engineers gradually developed innovations in manufacturing methods and also in the products themselves. Their efforts were stimulated by two successive influxes of American high-end machine tools, first around 1939 and again during the Marshall Plan (1948–1953). However, much more attention must be directed to the German influence during the Vichy period when, under the tutelage of German firms, French engineers and workers were obliged to adopt new technologies. This paper focuses on how they perceived their future with these newly acquired capabilities. The story begins in 1939 and ends in 1958, when the European Common Market commenced and the Fourth Republic collapsed. The sources are governmental research documents and annual reports of leading mechanical engineering firms in the Paris region, conserved chiefly in the Archives of Crédit Lyonnais. We begin with a quantitative outline.

2 The Importance of the Paris Region to French Mechanical Engineering

French industrial statistics traditionally focus on upstream industries like energy and raw materials and neglect downstream industries, so coherent quantitative data for the production of machines are unavailable before the late 1960s. The quantity

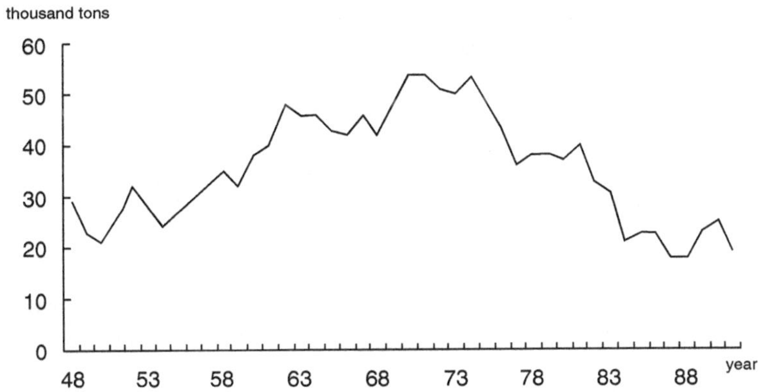

Fig. 4.1 Production of machine tools in France (Sources: *Annuaire rétrospectif de la France. Séries longues 1945–1986*, Paris, 1990. *Annuaire de statistique industrielle* 1987–1991)

of national production measured by weight dates back to 1948 only for machine tools (Fig. 4.1). After a growth phase during the 1950s, general prosperity in this branch continued until the early 1970s. Growth started with the Korean War boom of 1951–1952 and expanded constantly from 1955 to 1962, except for a short interruption during the 1958 political crisis. Tariff reductions brought brief stagnation until 1965. Rapid growth was re-ignited in 1966. Despite the revolt of May 1968, production peaked in 1971 and stayed at a plateau until the 1974 oil crisis. Thereafter it shrank, falling sharply after the 1980s. These fluctuations mirror many other branches of machinery production.

The industrial census of 1962 (INSEE 1967) shows the importance of Parisian factories to post-war growth. Despite the central government's persistent industrial relocation policy, the workforce in many branches of mechanical engineering remained concentrated around Paris. Of the 2.05 million workers employed in France's mechanical engineering sector (industrial classification 2), 762,135 (37.2%) worked in and around Paris (Ile-de-France), followed by the Rhône-Alpes region (234,199). Among nine sub-categories of mechanical engineering, shipbuilding (number 25) was the only one in which the Paris region did not rank first. Subcategories other than shipbuilding can be aggregated into four fields: general machines (industrial classifications 20–24; 998,251 workers nationally), transport machines (classifications 25–27; 588,913), electric machines (classification 28; 344,470) and precision machines (classification 29; 119,662). The percentages for the Paris region were 27.0%, 43.5%, 51.2% and 50.5%, respectively. In 1962 while most large provincial assembly plants for automobiles and home appliances were still in preparation, factories in and around Paris manufactured both capital goods and consumer durables. Nonetheless, as the share of these four fields in the Paris region comprised 35.4%, 33.6%, 23.1% and 7.9% respectively, it is clear that 'general machines' remained the main activity of these factories.

Figures by *département* show that most of these factories were located in the Seine *département*, which includes the City of Paris, with two *départements* of the

Paris region (Seine-et-Marne and Seine-et-Oise) having very few. The 1962 industrial census cites no figures for the distribution of these factories within the Seine *département* itself. Fortunately, periodicals published by the Seine *département* contain data on this subject for a period slightly before 1962 (Préfecture de la Seine 1958). The industrial classification differs from that of the 1962 census, but the pre-1962 censuses included mechanical engineering under the more general category 'metallurgy and machines'. In the Seine *département*, 379,054 workers were employed in this category in 1945 and 570,793 in 1958, a 50.6% increase during those 13 years. Of these 570,793 workers in 1958, 223,995 worked in Paris proper and 346,898 in its suburban *communes*. The 191,739 worker increase between 1945 and 1958 includes 82,055 Parisians and 109,684 suburban workers. At first glance, growth in the suburbs was impressive. But figures show that in 1945, 237,214 already worked in the suburbs versus 141,840 in Paris itself. In other words, growth in Paris (57.9%) exceeded that of the suburbs (46.7%). Therefore, factories in Paris retained their dynamism during the 1950s and probably into the early 1960s. The production system constructed in Paris during the late 1930s was the main force behind the development of French mechanical engineering during the first half, at least, of the *Trente Glorieuse* (1944–1973).

3 Parisian Machine-Makers and World War II

In earlier papers I have clarified the way in which rearmament during the second half of the 1930s boosted the process of reorganising mechanical engineering in the Paris region (Nakajima 1993, 1998). Those papers focused on three points. First, the remnants of armament production dispersed in the Paris region during World War I, which had been a deadweight against innovation by Parisian machine-makers before 1935, evolved into an important factor in their dynamism (Frankenstein 1982). Second, aircraft engine production became the leading technological branch of the region, and grinding machines imported from the United States enabled Parisian manufacturers to meet demand from the French Air Force for precision work. Third, notwithstanding this period of prosperity, Parisian machine manufacturers remained indifferent to the high-end metal-cutting technologies already employed in American and large German firms, such as cemented carbide bits, because individual firms did not have sufficient production levels.

After the war began, the rearmament boom in the Paris region accelerated until the Armistice of June 1940. The rush of military orders encouraged inter-firm relations among manufacturers. The government quickly established wartime production schemes so as to avoid the disturbances experienced at the beginning of World War I. As a result, armament production soon reached the expected volume in most cases. Initially, small machine shops agglomerated in Paris found it hard to share and rapidly execute military orders that were both huge and urgent. Archives of the *Groupe des Industries Métallurgiques, Mécaniques et Connexées de la Région Parisienne* (GIMM), conserved in the *Archives Nationales* (carton 39AS 212), testify to efforts by the staff of this regional trade association to solve this problem. From 14 September 1939 to 7 June 1940, it used the telephone to transmit more than 400 military orders from government to manufacturers, from assemblers to suppliers and from finishers to intermediate processors. Urgent military orders helped this trade association to weave a thick *tissu industriel* in the region.

After the Armistice, Germany occupied northern France, including Paris. German leaders were unable to adopt a coherent policy concerning French wartime production. Fritz Sauckel argued that the system should be destroyed and all machines and skilled workers transferred to Germany. Albert Speer insisted that it should be conserved and fully employed in supplying Germans with civilian goods and in supplementing domestic military production if possible. Both policies were executed side by side. Thus, the only way most mechanical engineering firms in the Paris region could survive was to be designated as German wartime plants ('*Rü-Betrieb*' or more fully '*S-Betrieb*') so that they could secure orders from the Occupation Authority and therefore be entitled to share in the distribution of energy and raw materials. If workers needed to be commandeered to Germany to satisfy the *service de travail obligatoire* (STO), French firms chose young and relatively untrained workers so as to retain the veterans in their own plants. This 'collaboration' with Germany remains a delicate problem for French historians. Until recently, they tended to rely on documents from the '*épuration*' proceedings written after the war even though these exaggerate the efforts of French industrialists at 'resistance' and 'sabotage'.

Rousso and Margairaz argue that production during the Vichy period must have been low given the shortages of energy and steel. Therefore even if much of the sabotage attributed to French industrialists is fictitious, they would still not have been able to satisfy all of the demand from Germany (Rousso and Margairaz 1992). However, statistics for coal and steel production during this period are unreliable because of widespread illegal trade. In fact, through his research in the Archives of the Occupation Authority conserved in Freiburg, Radtke-Delacor (2001) reveals the healthy state of French military production during the Vichy period.

As far as the Paris region is concerned, Rousselier-Fraboulet has examined the limited prosperity of the mechanical engineering industry in Saint-Denis under the Occupation and concluded that German military authority and German tutelary firms had a negative influence on French firms (Roussellier-Fraboulet 1998). But it must be acknowledged that mechanical engineering in Saint Denis, like other communes around northern Paris, was concentrated on heavy industrial machines, a sector where there had been stiff competition with both German and large northern French firms since the late nineteenth century. This explains part of the difficulty experienced by firms in Saint Denis. The southern and western *communes*, where the automobile and aircraft industries were located, present a quite different picture.

The Ministry of National Production created by the Vichy government conducted an industrial census after 1941 (Volle 1982). For the first time in French history, it tried to grasp directly, for each industrial establishment, the type of product, the total output, the number of workers and the level of energy consumption. The census remained incomplete because of wartime social paralysis, and the results of

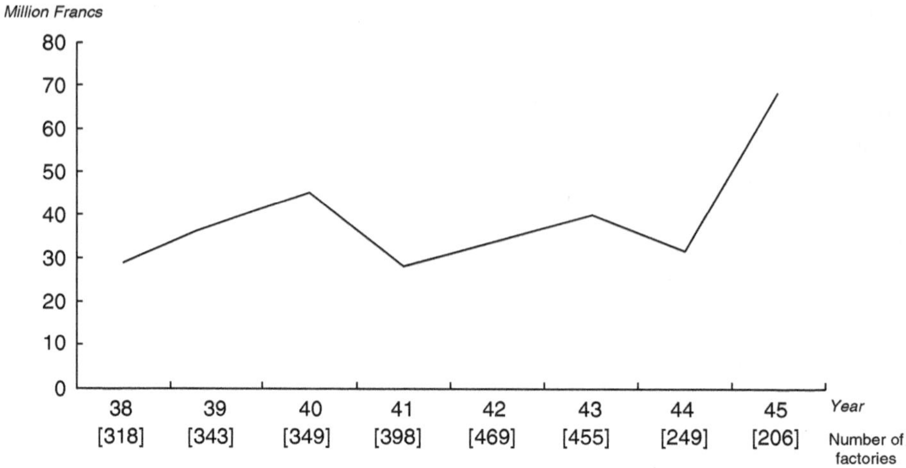

Fig. 4.2 Average yearly output of metalworking factories in the Seine département 1938–1945 (Source: Archives Nationales F12 9507–9531)

aggregation were not published. But individual bulletins classed by *département* and establishment indicate a rough picture of regional industrial development. Bulletins of the Seine *département* are conserved in the *Archives Nationales* (cartons F12 9507–9531). About one-fifth out of the 2243 bulletins related to the mechanical engineering and machine parts establishments in the area contain at least partial figures for annual output from 1938 to 1945. The calculation of yearly averages (Fig. 4.2) suggests that for 1941–1943 activity remained at 1938 levels, and that the paralysis of 1944 was not critical. The figures might have been padded because this census was connected to the distribution of energy and raw materials, but neither that possibility nor the existence of wartime inflation, produce any substantial change in the general image of prosperity.

We confirmed this view through precise examination of primary establishments in the region. The following factories were chosen: Gnome et Rhône and Hispano-Suiza for aircraft engines, Rateau for steam turbines, Compagnie Electro-Mecanique (CEM) for dynamos, and Société d'outillage mécanique et d'usinage d'artillerie (SOMUA) for vehicles and machine tools (Fig. 4.3). The prosperity of Gnome et Rhône as a manufacturer of aircraft engines was so eminent that its graph requires a special vertical axis (on the right). The number of workers at each factory in 1942 was 16,474 in Gnome et Rhône, 6559 in Hispano-Suiza, 1877 in Rateau, 1283 in CEM and 1523 in SOMUA. Although the number of workers at CEM declined to 1181 in 1943, employment at Rateau and SOMUA rose to 2076 and 2429 respectively. In the 1946 and 1947 annual reports of these firms, their directors looked back on the wartime experience and noted that shortage of energy and raw materials had not been severe except during some months of 1944. In sum, it is probable that the prosperity that resulted from the inter-firm relationships created before 1940 in order to facilitate rearmament continued, and even expanded, in the Vichy period.

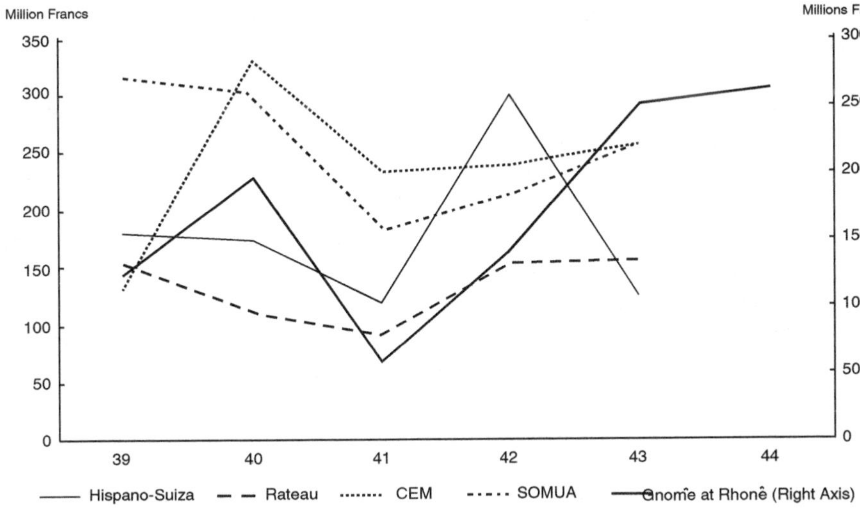

Fig. 4.3 Yearly output of major firms 1939–1944 (*Sources*: Archives Nationales F12 9507–9531)

Future research in the Freiburg and Potsdam archives of the German Occupation Authority might verify this hypothesis.

4 Parisian Machine-Makers During the Cold War and the Creation of the Common Market

Mioche (1985, 2004) has studied the post-war growth of the mechanical engineering industry, especially machine-tool production, to determine why French post-war economic plans did not fully include mechanical engineering. On the basis of interviews with André Garanger, former chief secretary of the trade association known as *Syndicat Français des Constructeurs de Machines Outils*, Mioche argues that an underlying atmosphere of narrow-minded corporatism and dislike of government intervention kept French machine-tool makers from participating in the Monnet Plan, and that their reluctance caused a delay in modernisation and therefore led to the decline of French mechanical engineering (Garanger 1960). The slight subjectivity of his viewpoint does not harm the plausibility of this argument in the long run, although it cannot fully explain the actual growth of the industry from the early 1950s until the mid-1960s.

Three points must be added to his conclusions. First, as the Monnet plan sought mainly to restore infrastructure and assure speedy supplies of coal and steel, it was natural for the Planning Agency to place initial dependence on ready-made American machines instead of embarking on the expensive and time-consuming modernisation of French machine-tool production. Second, massive imports of American machines remained rare except for some up-to-date machines used in the automobile and aircraft industry. This was because French machine-tool makers succeeded in satisfying national demand soon after the war. Third, the second and third economic plans encouraged machine-tool production, modest as it was, and even before that governmental measures (such as tax exemptions and direct investment schemes) existed to promote the industry (Nakajima 2015a).

In any event, after the post-war paralysis mechanical engineers in the Paris region generally enjoyed profitable conditions during reconstruction, the Cold War and colonial wars. Following the strategy prepared during the Vichy period, they reinvested in order to enter new and promising fields such as automobiles and aircraft, home electrical appliances, office machinery, and food processing. At the start of the mass consumption age, they stood ready to produce consumer durables and ready-made light machines and to expand their plant capabilities. Their initiatives reactivated the previously noted production network of small firms dispersed in and around Paris. Owing to the mediations of GIMM, the *tissu industriel* thickened further, not only in the 10th and 11th *arrondissements* of Paris but also in the eastern, northern and north-western suburbs, where small metalworking shops endeavoured to increase the quantity and quality of their production capabilities to meet the expected massive and strict orders for machine parts. As a result, the system of inter-firm division of labour was further refined.

Three unexpected incidents hampered these manufacturers. Sales of civilian goods during the late 1950s stagnated as France became bogged down in the Algerian War, and inflation and heavy taxes hindered investment. Inauguration of the Common Market heightened competition with West Germany during the 1960s, as well as with Italy, which had adopted almost the same industrial strategy as France. An even more crucial point was that the United States, Britain and Germany had begun trials in the use of numerical controls in metal processing during the 1950s, while the Parisian tradition of skilled manual labour prevented French industrialists from implementing this new technology. During the 1960s, this backwardness was hidden behind the quantitative expansion of the industry.

Thus, mechanical engineering gradually declined in the Paris region after the 1973 oil crisis. Many manufacturers transferred plants to the countryside or simply disappeared. Most surviving factories in the region were absorbed by large automobile and aircraft enterprises. The agglomeration of small metalworking shops in the 10th and 11th *arrondissements* of Paris was lost, and traditional inter-firm relationships as well as the subtle division of labour among firms had ceased to function by the end of the century.

5 The Vicissitudes Experienced by Primary Enterprises

The evolution of the mechanical engineering industry in the Paris region can be traced by examining documents belonging to the principal firms in each sub-sector. The analysis needs to be divided into two parts: products and production processes.

The following sketches are based on the annual reports and proposals for financing conserved in the *Archives Historiques du Crédit Lyonnais*: *Documents d'Études Économiques et Financières* Cartons 52380 (Hispano-Suiza), 61051 and 65677 (Gnome et Rhône), 49811 and 52295 (Rateau), 52401 and 59827 (Alsthom), 52407 and 59832 (CEM), 52409 and 60996 (SGCM), 52357 (Marinoni), 52344 (Aster), 52340 (Bariquand et Marre), 50715 (SOMUA), 52346 (Cazeneuve) and 52353 and 77125 (Huré). Documents conserved at the *Archives Nationales*, especially series 122AQ (SOMUA), were also consulted.

5.1 The Evolution of Product Policy

5.1.1 Aircraft Engines

Large manufacturers of aircraft engines were the technical forerunners of mechanical engineering in the Paris region. During the early years of reciprocating engines, globally dominant firms like Wright, Pratt & Whitney (P&W) and Rolls-Royce were challenged by three French makers: Gnome et Rhône, Hispano-Suiza and Lorraine-Dietrich. The first two firms operated parts foundries in western suburban Paris and assembly plants in the south end of the city itself. Before World War II, manufacturer Rateau (see below) secretly began studying jet engine technology. During the Occupation, all these factories were under the tutelage of German firms such as Daimler-Benz and BMW. It is certain that some of the high-end machine-tools imported from the United States before the occupation were transferred to Germany, but most equipment remained in Paris and was even augmented up until 1944 to maximise production of German aircraft engines. Gnome et Rhône was nationalised for this reason after the war, becoming the Société Nationale d'Étude et de Construction des Moteurs d'Aviation (SNECMA). French firms continued to study jet engines but could not catch up with their American and British rivals. SNECMA became a licensee of P&W and Hispano-Suiza of Rolls-Royce. The failure of the Concorde obliged Hispano-Suiza to be absorbed by SNECMA in 1968. French aircraft engine manufacturers withdrew from the front ranks and survived on orders from the French Air Force. However, the SNECMA factory, transferred in 1962 to Corbeil in a distant southern suburb of Paris, continued to be a cradle for skilled metalworkers of the highest level.

5.1.2 Industrial Motors

During the 1930s, the golden age of steam engines passed and steam turbines for electric power plants became the main sources of industrial energy. The use of diesel engines expanded among smaller users. To promote French production of big turbines and dynamos, Alstom (originally Alsthom) was created in 1927 in Belfort in eastern France as a joint venture of Compagnie Française Thomson-Houston and

Société Alsacienne de Constructions Mécaniques. Besides the main Belfort factory, Alsthom had two big factories in the Paris region. Soon it ranked alongside Schneider (Le Creuzot) as a representative French heavy machine manufacturer, constructing electric power plants and locomotives. It initially copied large General Electric dynamos, but during the 1930s, it stood on its own. Growth continued during the war. As the construction of electric power plants became less profitable because of international competition, it launched into small motors, widened its product line, and absorbed some major heavy machine manufacturers in the mid-1950s.

Founded in the early twentieth century in La Courneuve in the northern suburbs of Paris, Rateau was a world-famous turbine manufacturer for electric power plants and large ships and turbo-chargers for reciprocating engines. As noted above, it began studying jet engines in the late 1930s. In the 1950s, it entered the field of nuclear power plants, but as international competition intensified, the company confronted problems of production capacity. Alsthom absorbed it in 1972. CEM in Le Bourget, also in the northern suburbs of Paris, manufactured middle-range dynamos and electric locomotives. In the 1950s, it too faced competition and turned to smaller dynamos and motors. In 1957, it absorbed laundry machine manufacturer Konor in Reims. That venture failed, and CEM was also absorbed by Alsthom in 1985. Société Générale de Construction Mécanique (SGCM) in La Courneuve was created in the late nineteenth century from a merger of five steam engine manufacturers in the Paris region. In the inter-war years, it became a licensee of the German diesel engine manufacturer M.A.N. During the period of pre-war rearmament, it strengthened its relationship with the French Navy. After the war it became a subsidiary of Penhoët Shipyard in Saint-Nazaire, specialising in submarine motors and dynamos.

Thus, after a short period of prosperity, some major motor manufacturers in the Paris region were absorbed by Alsthom, and the others survived thanks to military orders.

5.1.3 Varied Industrial Machines

Traditionally, the mechanical engineering industry around Paris excelled in a variety of products. Here we will focus on three of them: printing machines, gas pumps and office machinery.

Marinoni, a global pioneer in rotary presses, failed to diversify in the twentieth century and was absorbed by Edouard-Lambert in the 1930s. During the Vichy period, groaning under the tutelage of German firms, it created new models of rotary presses and offset printers. These new products sold well after the war, and Marinoni was revived as one of Europe's main manufacturers of printing machines.

Aster was an old manufacturer of small diesel engines in the northern suburbs of Paris. Facing keen competition from German firms after World War II, it began to make pumps for gas stations and gained great success.

The case of Bariquand et Marre is more impressive. Originally a manufacturer of clippers for sheep and human haircuts situated in the 11th *arrondissement* of Paris, it made machine guns during World War I. In the inter-war period, it began to process precision machine parts. During the Vichy period, German tutelary firms stole its precious industrial property: product plans, ideas and trademarks. The Cold War separated it from its markets in Eastern Europe. To overcome these difficulties, Bariquand et Marre jumped into the field of office machinery, buying US patents and making calculators and statistical machines. Its products enjoyed a good reputation for a while, and it became an emblematic French office machinery manufacturer. Later, its small electric computer Logabax challenged Nixdorf in European markets. Menaced by competition from IBM, it was absorbed by Olivetti. Many machine shops in Paris followed similar patterns.

5.1.4 Machine Tools

Société d'Outillage Mécanique et d'Usinage d'Artillerie (SOMUA), in the north Parisian suburb of Saint-Ouen, was a major French manufacturer of machine tools. It originated as Société Française de Machines-Outils, the creation of automobile assemblers in 1907. Within 5 years, the business broke down, and Schneider bought its factory. As the change of name shows, the new firm made not only large machine tools but also military trucks, tanks and artillery tractors. In 1954, trucks accounted for two thirds of its sales, with machine tools and Marinoni offset printers comprising the remainder. The next year, truck production was separated from SOMUA and merged with Latil and the truck section of Renault to form Société Anonyme de Véhicules Industriels et d'Équipement Mécaniques (actually Renault Véhicules Industriels). The machine-tool section of SOMUA merged in 1963 with H. Ernault, a prominent lathe manufacturer in Nantes also under the financial control of Schneider. The new firm was named H. Ernault-SOMUA.

Several smaller machine-tool manufacturers played an important role. Cazeneuve, one of the most distinctive of them, manufactured small lathes in Saint-Denis, a northern suburb of Paris. Weakened by the war, it detoured into making semi-automatic lathes. While German manufacturers launched successively heavier special machine tools of high precision, Cazeneuve concentrated on small universal lathes. Light, high-speed, easy-to-use and inexpensive, Cazeneuve's lathes allowed a sufficient degree of precision in processing, fitting well into the Parisian small metalworking shop agglomeration of the 1950s. Cazeneuve was absorbed by H. Ernault-SOMUA in the 1980s. According to *La Machine-Outil Française* (number 75, March 1953), Huré, a milling machine manufacturer in Bagneux in the southern suburbs of Paris, adopted product strategies similar to Cazeneuve. Maintaining the tradition of Parisian metalworking, these smaller firms constituted the base of the mechanical engineering industry surrounding Paris.

All these cases show that Parisian mechanical engineers adapted and developed products speedily as their industrial circumstances evolved. They did not lose vigour until the mid-1960s and provided a solid base for French industrial growth. Nearly the same adaptability can be observed in the sphere of production techniques.

5.2 Technical Innovations in Metal Processing

This section surveys two great innovations of the period and then examines some smaller but equally important improvements.

5.2.1 Grinding Machines and Cemented Carbide Tool Bits

Invented in the United States at the beginning of the twentieth century, large universal grinding machines are indispensable in the mass production of high-precision machine parts made of hard steel. Large machine tools of this type were introduced in France during World War I, but diffusion was slow until the mid-1930s in all sectors except the production of automobile engines. As rearmament started, the government encouraged French manufacturers to make universal grinding machines, but time was so limited that the main users—aircraft engine makers—were obliged to rely on American grinders. As was explained above, many machines thus imported were used to mass-produce German aircraft engines in the Vichy period. But maintaining the American and German grinders gave Parisian machine-tool manufacturers ample occasion to become acquainted with this new technology. After the war, their production of grinding machines expanded so rapidly that in the early 1950s the second economic plan could rely on French grinders, the only exception being some specialised machines used by the automobile industry.

Invented in Germany in the 1920s, cemented carbide tool bits were improved in the United States in the 1930s. But as French metalworking factories, especially in the Paris region, made most products to order, they generally remained indifferent to this new technology since it was suited to mass-production. Under German occupation, Parisian metalworkers were obliged to handle these new tool bits for the first time. According to a SOMUA training report of May 1942 conserved in the Crédit Lyonnais Archives, so many French skilled metalworkers broke the tips of cemented carbide tool bits that the trainer did not know what to do. This was because cemented carbide tool bits had to be handled differently from traditional carbon steel and high-speed steel bits. Therefore, training of STO workers by German firms in France and Germany must have played an important role in preparing for post-war French industrial development. According to a series of reports in *La Machine-Outil Française* (numbers 61–65, from December 1951 to March 1952), post-war production of cemented carbide tool bits expanded rapidly in France to meet automobile industry demand.

5.2.2 The Diffusion of 'Light' Universal Machine-Tools

As was explained above, some machine-tool manufacturers in occupied Paris were secretly able to study the 'light' universal machine tools that were suited to the French market. Although compact and cheap, they worked with speed and precision. Moreover, a small but powerful electric motor was attached directly to each machine, facilitating the rational layout of factories. These machines contributed to post-war innovations in French mechanical engineering. In the 1940s, the age of the machine tools used in French factories was said to average 25 years. This figure must be exaggerated, but it is certain that in France, especially around Paris, the market in used machine tools prospered. Jumbles of power transmission belts and outdated simple machine-tools were a common sight in the small old machine shops agglomerated in Paris. This poor equipment was traditionally supplemented by the high manual skill of Parisian metalworkers. Although this network of independent small shops encouraged flexible manufacturing, the system in its original form was not capable of producing large production lots requiring high precision. In the prosperous early 1950s, 'light' universal machine tools were diffused among these small shops, and they could barely catch up with the age of mass-production (Salmon 1956, 1958). In the late 1960s, large factories manufacturing automobiles and household appliances began to appear in the farther suburbs of Paris. By then, the traditional network of small machine shops in and near Paris, although diminished in efficiency, constituted the base for French industrial growth.

5.2.3 Intermediate Technologies

Less spectacular technical changes constituted the majority of innovations in the region. The recent case of small metalworking shops in Ota Ward in southern Tokyo shows that the accumulation of commonplace inventions is sometimes more important than epoch-making technological innovations in constructing efficient production systems. These inventions are called 'intermediate technologies'. Examples also appeared in small Parisian metalworking shops during the 1950s and 1960s.

Ernest Gaucher, a graduate of the *Ecole des Arts et Métiers* of Paris, specialised in factory layouts. One of his books concerns the machine repair shop of a large dairy plant near Paris (Gaucher 1953). The shop was in complete disorder after the war. Gaucher first made the accurate calculation of costs possible by introducing a coherent system to invoice machine parts. Then he sold out all of the central power distribution system using a large electric motor, ceiling power shafts and transmission belts, and in exchange he attached a small electric motor equipped with a gearbox to each machine tool. As a result, it was possible to introduce a rational layout of the machines in the shop in what is called a 'convenient direct motor drive system'. Through these measures and with almost no additional costs, he quadrupled the efficiency of the repair shop. There are many similar reports in professional journals of the period (Borlant 1950; Anonymous 1950).

Another example is a graduation thesis (*mémoire d'ingénieur OST*) of the *Ecole des Arts et Métiers* of Paris (Rose 1966). Bernard Rose chose as his subject the safety management of his parents' metal pressing shop in the eastern suburbs of Paris. Collaborating with skilled workers in the shop, he created an apparatus for automatic shifting of the raw material, namely steel belts. The apparatus sold well and became a profitable product of the shop.

These small inventions attract little attention compared with big innovations like universal grinding machines and cemented carbide tool bits, but the prosperity of the mechanical engineering industry in the Paris region in the first half of the *Trente Glorieuse* largely depended on them. The second case above, which transformed a simple processing shop into a machine manufacturer, also exemplifies the growth in the level of the inter-firm division of labour.

6 The Continued Existence of Small Shops

There was no extensive research into the network of small metalworking shops surrounding the Paris region before 1960. After Jacques Houssiaux and others introduced the stratified profit rates theory of Joseph Steindl in the late 1950s, researchers became interested in the positive aspects of small firms (Houssiaux 1957). In the 1960s, geographers and sociologists studied agglomeration, which led to the detailed monographs of Françoise Lanoiselée-Quirel and Alain Champaux in the 1970s (Lanoiselée-Quirel 1975; Champaux 1976).

Among the studies that appeared in the 1960s is one by Serge Goldberg (Goldberg 1965). Under the sponsorship of the *Institut d'Aménagement et d'Urbanisme de la Région Parisienne*, from 1963 to 1964 this sociologist interviewed 8 large assemblers and 54 parts suppliers employing fewer than 50 workers in the Paris region (Fig. 4.4). Apparently he was not totally unaffected by the customary negative view of small firms, as he classified suppliers according to the weight of their main trade partner as 'dependent' and 'independent' firms, and showed more respect for the latter. Nonetheless, his results show how the production network functioned.

Most suppliers were new (more than half arose after the war), their directors were young (two-thirds were under 50 years of age), their legal structure was modern (two-thirds were *société anonyme*), and 47 out of 54 suppliers indicated that their businesses were expanding. Shops were built on borrowed land in more than half the cases. Equipment was new, and many directors intended to introduce the newest machines. In most cases more than half the workers were highly skilled, and some suppliers subcontracted part of their work to smaller firms. Most directors and workers were autodidacts. There were only nine certificated engineers and two officially skilled workers (holding the title of CAP, *Certificat d'Aptitude Professionnelle*).

Many shops were in the western suburbs of Paris but many had also stayed in the city, especially in the east end (10th, 11th, 18th and 19th *arrondissements*) where rents were already high. This point was also suggested by the research of two geographers (Beaujeu-Garnier and Bastié 1967). What advantages compensated for the high rents in these areas? According to the interviews, important factors were not only the availability of skilled labour and raw materials, but also the fact that the proximity of shops in related branches facilitated business operations. For example, they could share large orders and rely on neighbours for supplementary processing. These conveniences were crucial to the flexible production that characterised this agglomeration of metalworking shops. As cited above, such inter-firm relations

Fig. 4.4 Assemblers and suppliers in and near Paris 1963 (interviewed by Goldberg) (Sources: Serge Goldberg, "La sous-traitance dans l'industrie des métaux," *Cahiers de l'Institut d'Aménagement et d'Urbanisme de la Région Parisienne*, Vol. 2, 1965)

began to be formalised by trade associations and large assemblers, but the situation stayed amorphous in the first half of the 1960s, and even the smallest shops had the chance to catch some of the informal orders which crowded into the east end.

What is particularly interesting is that most orders were verbal agreements without documents – for fiscal reasons, certainly – but promptness and flexibility of business were no less important. Orders often took the form of rough sketches and prototypes. Goldberg argues that these confused dealings show a lack of rationality among small metalworking shops. The business occasioned frequent legal disputes, and sanctions aimed at preventing the exploitation of sub-contractors became legal in the 1970s.

But this amorphous situation can be explained in a more positive way. The rapid expansion of assembly plants may have been the cause behind the 'dependence' of suppliers on their main partner. The bewildering changes in products could have necessitated promptness and flexibility in the supply of parts. This view shows that apparently irrational trade customs can contain elements of rationality, as is certainly the case in the more recent example of Tokyo's Ota Ward. This would explain why the symbiosis of suburban large factories and versatile small metalworking shops in the City of Paris, as well as the interdependence between small firms, occurred after 1935 and continued to intensify until the early 1960s. In fact, these relations were indispensable factors in French industrial growth in the first half of the *Trente Glorieuse*.

7 Conclusion

Throughout the 1960s, large plants manufacturing automobiles and household appliances were independently established in the countryside, each one manufacturing its own machine parts. By means of tax exemptions and subsidiaries, the de Gaulle government induced small metalworking shops to merge and exit Paris. Some small firms rationalised and found new positions in the production system led by large assemblers. Others survived in niche markets, serving the military or nuclear power stations, for example. Others still disappeared. Thus, the east end of Paris ceased to function as a metalworking centre. Finally the age of mass-production began, and French industry grew faster than ever as a result of the oligopolistic competition between multinational manufacturers.

However, when, in the 1980s, the increase in average income resulted in the individualisation of markets, 'lean production' emerged, and assemblers were obliged to rebuild a flexible external supply system of parts and materials. On that occasion, they remarked on the importance of what they had lost in the 1960s. They had to re-introduce from Japan and Korea the system of supply chains renovated by numerical control technology (Nakajima 2015b). However, as French workers have been reduced to simple machine operators (Nakajima 2005), the system remains inefficient compared with Asia, where workers have more diverse skills. The resurgence of French industry requires more detailed studies of the history of mechanical engineering in Paris.

References

Anonymous. 1950. Conseils généraux pour l'installation et l'entretien des moteurs électriques. *La Machine Moderne* 488.

Beaujeu-Garnier, Jacqueline, and Jean Bastié, eds. 1967. *Atlas de Paris et de la Région Parisienne*. Paris: Berger-Levrault.

Borlant, Roger. 1950. L'application de la commande électrique des moteurs à la machine-outil. *La Machine-Ouril Française* 41–43.

Champaux, Alain. 1976. Développement des entreprises de sous-traitance du secteur découpage-emboutissage. Mémoire pour le DEA, Université Paris I (Unpublished thesis).

Frankenstein, Robert. 1982. *Le prix du réarmement français 1935–1939*. Paris: Publications de la Sorbonne.

Garanger, André. 1960. *Petite histoire d'une grande industrie*. Neuilly-sur-Seine: Société d'édition pour la mécanique et la machine-outil.

Gaucher, Ernest. 1953. *L'organisation d'un atelier de mécanique*. Paris: Éditions d'Organization.

Goldberg, Serge. 1965. La sous-traitance dans l'industrie des métaux. *Cahiers de l'Institut d'Aménagement et d'Urbanisme de la Région Parisienne* 2.

INSEE. 1967. *Recensement de l'industrie 1963. Résultats pour 1962. Série structurelle. Vol. 4 : Tous établissements. Résultats par régions*. Paris: Imprimerie nationale.

Lanoiselée-Quirel, Françoise. 1975. La stratégie des moyennes entreprises de mécanique. Thèse pour le doctorat, Université Paris I (Unpublished thesis).

Mioche, Philippe. 1985. Les difficultés de la modernisation dans le cas de l'industrie française de la machine outil, 1941–1953. *EUI Working Paper* 85/168.

———. 2004. La triple malédiction de l'industrie de la machine-outil en France. In *Autour de l'industrie, histoire et patrimoine: Mélanges offerts à Denis Woronoff*, ed. Jean-François Belhoste et al. Paris: CHEF.

Nakajima, Toshikatsu. 1985. Industrie mécanique à Paris 1847–1914. Thèse du doctorat de troisième cycle. Université de Paris IV (Unpublished thesis).

———. 1987. Les machines françaises aux expositions internationales 1851–1911. *KSU Economic and Business Review* (Kyoto) 14.

———. 1993. L'impact de la guerre de 1914–1918 sur l'industrie mécanique de la Région Parisienne. *Histoire Economie et Société* 12 (4).

———. 1998. Crise et croissance de l'industrie mécanique de la Région Parisienne 1918–1939. In *Les entreprises et leurs réseaux*, ed. Michèle Merger and Dominique Barjot. Paris: Presses de l'Université Paris-Sorbonne.

———. 2005. Formation des mécaniciens dans la Région Parisienne au milieu du XXe siècle. *Bulletin de la Société franco-japonaise de gestion* 25.

———. 2015a. French Economic Plans and the Mechanical Engineering Industry in the Paris Region, 1953–1974. In *France-Japon, regards croisés*, ed. Patrick Fridenson and Dominique Barjot. Paris: Presses de l'Université Paris-Sorbonne.

———. 2015b. Le transfert de la technologie des machines-outils français au Japon (1952–1962). In *Le monde du génie industriel au XXe siècle : autour de Pierre Béziet et des machines-outils*, ed. Serge Benoît and Alain P. Michel. Belfort: Pôle éditorial de l'Université de technologie de Belfort-Montbéliard.

Préfecture de la Seine. 1958. *Conjoncture économique du département*, 4e trimestre.

Radtke-Delacor, Arne. 2001. Produire pour le Reich. Les commandes allemandes à l'industrie française (1941–1944). *Vingtième siècle*, avril-juin.

Rose, Bernard. 1966. Organisation, rôle et action du service Méthode dans une grande entreprise de découpage, emboutissage, tôlerie et fabrication de ressorts, travaillant à façon dans la Région Parisienne. Mémoire d'ingénieur OST, Conservatoire Nationale des Arts et Métiers (Unpublished).

Roussellier-Fraboulet, Danièle. 1998. *Les entreprises sous l'occupation. Le monde de la métallurgie à Saint-Denis*. Paris: Éditions du CNRS.

Rousso, Henry and Michel Margairaz. 1992. Vichy, la guerre et les entreprises. In *Histoire Economie et Société* 11 (3) (equally in: Henry Russo, *Vichy. L' événement, la mémoire, l'histoire*, Paris, Gallimard, 2001).

Salmon, Pierre. 1956. Les machines-outils d'usage général en face de l'automatisation. *La Machine Moderne* 568.

———. 1958. Les petites séries (Éditorial). *La Machine Moderne* 591.

Volle, Michel. 1982. *Histoire de la statistique industrielle*. Paris: Economica.

Part II
Book Reviews

Chapter 5
Review of Shūichi Takashima, *Toshi Kinkō no Kōchi Seiri to Chiiki Shakai: Tokyo-Setagaya no Kōgai Kaihatsu* (Urban Development and Local Communities in Interwar Tokyo)

Nihon Keizai Hyōronsha, Tokyo, 2013

Akinobu Numajiri

This book is an empirical investigation into land development in Japan based on a case study of the Tamagawa Zenen Land Readjustment Association that was active in a suburban area of Tokyo during the period before, during, and after the second world war. The author pays special attention to changes in the principles of social organization that the case study reveals.

In the introduction, the author explains that his focus lies on the way in which fundamental principles of a certain type of economic rationality can gain dominance in a society that is not completely based on capitalism, and thus lead to overall social stability. In other words, rather than accepting the inevitability of arable land readjustment projects, he examines the reasons why particular local communities consented to land readjustment, and the process by which they did so.

In Chapter 1, "Land readjustment and the development of residential land in the Tokyo suburbs", the author describes how developers, land providers and governing bodies in the Tokyo suburbs worked together to develop land in the period following the first world war. Their dealings were based on the assumption that any losses would be met by the price rises that would follow the readjustment of arable land. In one sense, the logic behind this meant that compensation for any debt that might occur was replaced by temporary profits that might not actually be realisable. On the other hand, the author points out that the result was a further advance in the commercialisation of land, which meant that it had economic rationality.

This is a translation of a book review that originally appeared in *Shakai Keizai Shigaku* 80(2) (August 2014), pp. 135–137.

A. Numajiri (✉)
College of Arts, Rikkyo University,
3-34-1, Nishi-ikebukuro, Toshima-ku, 171-8501 Tokyo, Japan
e-mail: numajiri@rikkyo.ac.jp

S. Baba (ed.), *Economic History of Cities and Housing*, Monograph Series of the Socio-Economic History Society, Japan, DOI 10.1007/978-981-10-4097-9_5

Chapter 2, "The formation of land readjustment associations and the order of local communities" gives the background to the formation of the Tamagawa Zenen Land Readjustment Association. The author shows that it can be seen as a response to the challenges presented by falling agricultural profits (the economic crisis facing individual farmers) and the activities of developers (the social crisis facing local communities). He emphasizes the following points: Partly because of the disparities that existed within different parts of the village, the process of adjustment was split into sections. This became a cause of tensions between different parts of the association. Further, in the areas where readjustment first began, the preexisting order of the area had a strong influence.

Chapter 3, "The beginning of land readjustment and the activities of the association in the eastern part of Tamagawa" is an analysis of what happened in the eastern part of Tamagawa, which was the first area to be readjusted. The community survived the process of compensation for those who had to move and the sales of association land, but management problems made it difficult to proceed further in other parts of the village.

Chapter 4, "Developments in the land readjustment project and changes in the activities of the association in the central and western parts of Tamagawa" examines the central and western areas that became the next target of readjustment. The author points out that agreement regarding both changes in the divisions between areas and the payment of compensation to those who had to move was reached through new, non-traditional, structures within the community. Developers were allowed to take part in the affairs of the association and while some friction occurred, the idea that land readjustment could bring profits as a result of increases in the price of land gained acceptance.

The concluding chapter, "Land readjustment and the shift in the principles behind the organization of communities", contains analyses of the members of the association and of the allocation of land throughout the territory that it covered. As it became harder for it to perform as an organisation based on traditional understandings of social order, the association came to agree with principles of value. At the same time, it also turned into a functional group. The author finishes this chapter by describing land readjustment in Tamagawa as an expression of the shift from modern to contemporary society. (There is a supplementary chapter at the end with the title "The hegemony of land readjustment.")

The reviewer's evaluation of the book is as follows:

1. One of the clear merits of this book is its utilisation of the primary materials relating to the Tamagawa Zenen Land Readjustment Association held by the Setagaya Museum of History in order to carry out empirical research into urban formation in the suburbs of Tokyo. The way in which the author has used accounts of meetings of the association, including actual quotations, is of particular interest because of the insights that this gives into the role of conflicts of interest and other elements in the discussions of committees and local meetings. As a result, in Chapters 3 and 4, the reader gains a vivid understanding of the response to the process of readjustment in different parts of Tamagawa. For

example, this approach helps to illustrate the changing attitude of association members towards developers and the effect of the great depression on the measures taken towards the sale of association land in different areas. Chapter 2 also provides valuable insights into the hitherto neglected aspect of the views taken by landowners resident in Tokyo. Indeed, this is probably the first piece of research to examine an association in the suburbs of Tokyo for the readjustment of arable land for the purpose of urban formation. Since it tackles a big association that represented a complete village unit, it is all the more valuable.

2. Further, the study presents a reassessment of the paradigms of modern and contemporary society from the point of view of economic history. This is another merit, especially since such attempts are uncommon. However, some aspects of the author's argument are hard to understand:

   (a) Some of the technical terms and concepts are not clearly defined. Key examples of this are expressions such as "*chiiki shakai chitsujo* (the order in local communities)", "*dentōteki shakai chitsujo* (traditional social order)" and "*dentōteki chiiki shakai chitsujo* (the traditional social order of local communities)". From the explanation beginning on p. 226, "the order in local communities" would seem to mean the social order of agricultural-based settlements within villages but there is no concrete explanation of what the traditional "order in local communities" in the late 1920s might be. The expression "*dentōteki* (traditional)" often includes the idea of a moral economy and is associated with pre-modern societies. However, in the interwar period that is covered by this book, the social structure is no longer "pre-modern" since the focus lies on landowners rather than ordinary peasants. In other words, the author needed to explain his concept of "the order in local communities" fully and give examples of the relationships between landowners and tenant farmers, the ties between landowners, landlords and those who rented housing, and the various connections related to land held in common.

   (b) Some of the evidence that the author gave to justify key points in his argument was not strong enough. The weakest part concerned his explanation of the point at which local communities accepted the principle of the monetary value of land. First, in Chapter 3 he tries to prove that in the eastern part of Tamagawa, rises in land price were not an important criterion. As evidence, he gives the fact that in one of the readjustment areas they calculated the amount of land that was moved at a 30% reduction and tried to suppress the rate of land decrease. He used this as evidence of the fact that "the idea that land could increase in value after readjustment" had not yet been internalised as a norm by local communities (p. 149). However, movements of land where he claims that the land decrease rate had been suppressed are recorded in the primary sources as movements after final surveys had been carried out. In other words, in cases where the association had carried out provisional replotting, the area of allotment was decided then, and the movements could be seen as settlements that were carried out as a result of final surveys after that. If this were the case, the target of the 30% reduction would be a minor adjustment after replotting. Since it is unclear whether or not provisional allotment was actually implemented, the reviewer may be labouring under a misapprehension, but the lack of any explanation regarding the quotation means that it is not possible to check which interpretation is correct. Further, the meeting is dated as October 1931, a period when land prices had fallen. Taken together with the fact that the plan was not actually carried out, it seems likely that this evidence cannot be taken as conclusive proof that the principle of the monetary value of land had not penetrated local communities.

A second weak point occurs in Chapter 4. Here, on the contrary, the issue is evidence of the acceptance by local communities of rates of decrease based on the principle of the monetary value of land and urban planning works that enforced this. Here the author points to discussions about the width of planned roads and the arguments made during disagreements about the establishment of garbage incineration plants and pig farms. He uses evidence such as petitions concerning the fall in land prices that will occur in the neighbourhood of incineration plants to prove that locally communities had come to accept the principle of the monetary value of land. The petitions certainly include expressions such as "from the viewpoint of the management of residential land", but the supporters of the petitions included the parents of children at the primary school, and it is not clear that they had grasped the concept of "the principle of the monetary value of land". With regard to the pig farm, he points to the fact that the minutes of the meeting include the idea that it will harm the development of the land and claims that "the use of the word 'harm' implied falling land prices" (p. 186), but this seems to be a somewhat farfetched claim. Rather, as the author himself admits, since the plan to establish a pig farm is a land use that is not appropriate to an urban area, it indicates the continued existence of farmers in this area. In view of the fact that about half of the allotment of land took place after the end of the war (pp. 212–213), it should not really be possible to come to conclusions about the shift to contemporary society unless the period from the beginning of the war until the post war reforms is also taken into consideration.

Finally, the reviewer would like to make a brief reply to criticisms that the author has made regarding his research. First, the author claims that Numajiri (2002) applied an a priori dualistic framework of "state = public" and "people = private" (p. 17) instead of emphasizing the fact that land readjustment projects were compulsory, and possessed dynamic elements. The reviewer accepts the compulsory element of these projects, and in later works has drawn attention to the facts of landownership and use. He intends to bring these works together in a monograph at a later date. Moreover, even in the work that the author cites (Numajiri 2002), he drew attention to the role of landowner-tenant relationships and human relationships controlled by local elites in land adjustment and the development of factory land, and pointed out that while different from the public sphere represented by national law they formed an alternate public sphere. In other words, the reviewer did not apply an a priori dualistic framework. In particular, he did not take the simplistic view that "people = private". The different perceptions of the reviewer and the author are fundamentally related to the arguments of Kawashima Takeyoshi, a representative postwar expert on civil law who pointed out the landowner-tenant relationship in Japan involved human ties that could not be separated from material ties (Kawashima 1987), in other words, that there was a gap between general perceptions of law and the understanding of "person" in the sense of the subjective actor envisaged by modern law. As a result, unlike the author, the reviewer considers that it is difficult to find elements of civic society in villages as administrative units in interwar Japan. It is for this reason that, as was mentioned above, he emphasizes the importance of including analysis of the period from the beginning of the war onwards, when cultivation rights gained legal strength. The reviewer has laid his arguments alongside the criticisms of the author and presents the points of difference, as he understands them. But he would like to end by saying that as well as being a significant work of local history, this book also presents a new way of approaching local communities and the historical paradigms of modern and contemporary society.

Postscript

Numajiri (2015) appeared after the publication of this book. One of the chapters, "Landowners and tenant farmers in the process of urban formation: a case study of Amagasaki city, Hyogo prefecture, 1937–1952", is included in the present volume. Since it includes an examination of the legal strengthening of cultivation rights referred to above, readers might like to consult it.

References

Kawashima, Takeyoshi. 1987. *Shinpan Shoyūken-hō no riron* [Theories of Ownership Law]. new ed. Tokyo: Iwanami Shoten.

Numajiri, Akinobu. 2002. *Kōjō ritchi to toshi keikaku* [Plant Location and City Planning]. Tokyo: Tokyo Daigaku Shuppankai.

———. 2015. *Sonraku kara mita shigaichi keisei* [The Process of Urban Formation as Seen from Rural Communities]. Tokyo: Nihon Keizai Hyōronsha.

Chapter 6
Review of Tadashi Nakano, Tatsuyuki Karasawa and Ichirō Michishige (eds), *18 Seiki no Igirisu Toshikūkan o Saguru: Toshi "Runesansu" ron Saikō* (Exploring Urban Space in Eighteenth-Century England: A Reappraisal of the Urban Renaissance Debate)

Tōsui Shobō, Tokyo, 2012

Minoru Yasumoto

Since 1989, Peter Borsay's *The English Urban Renaissance: Culture and Society in the Provincial Town, 1660–1770* has been influential in the study of modern British urban history. Inspired by his work, Tadashi Nakano, Ichiro Michishige and Tatsuyuki Karasawa, leading Japanese historians working in this field, in 2004 organized a study group to reappraise British urban history in the 'long' eighteenth century. They chose to focus on this era rather than the period of industrialization, the late-eighteenth and nineteenth centuries, which has tended to attract considerably more attention from British and Japanese scholars interested in the modern urban history of Britain.

This book is a result of the group's collaboration. Ten of its members, along with Penelope Corfield (from Royal Holloway, London) contribute papers, the topics of which range widely across modern English towns. The work displays extensive research and keen analysis. Parts of the research have already been reported in a panel discussion at the annual conference in 2009 of the Socio-Economic History Society of Japan. The following brief summaries of each contribution are intended

This is a translation of a book review that originally appeared in *Shakai Keizai Shigaku* 79(2) (August 2013), pp. 145–147.

M. Yasumoto (✉)
Faculty of Economics, Komazawa University, Tokyo 154-8525, Japan
e-mail: yasumoto@komazawa-u.ac.jp

S. Baba (ed.), *Economic History of Cities and Housing*, Monograph Series of the Socio-Economic History Society, Japan, DOI 10.1007/978-981-10-4097-9_6

to highlight what the authors identify as currently the most important questions confronting English urban history in the 'long' eighteenth century.

In her survey of research trends in British urban history since the middle of the last century, 'The State of Urban History: The British Case as Exemplar', Corfield points out that studies have always embraced a wide range of characteristics: economic, social, cultural, political, environmental, landscape, architectural, gender, leisure, and intellectual, as well as specific functions. This is because, as she asserts, British towns are urban 'palimpsests', with endless overlaps and re-usages over many different eras. Thus, the collected papers here follow the orthodox approach adopted by many British urban historians.

Nakano's overview of historical studies on British urban societies in the eighteenth century, as well as his reappraisal of the 'Urban Renaissance Debates', are excellent. Picking up from L.D. Schwartz and Jon Stobart, he notices an urban function providing inhabitants with a space for 'practical enlightenment', besides opportunities for widening scope for leisure, commodities for conspicuous consumption and services, and a life-style based on civility and politeness. Schwartz and Stobart identified 'residential leisure towns' by examining tax records for the proportion of households with male servants, symbolizing an urban renaissance with leisured and conspicuous consumption.

In a study of eighteenth-century British towns focusing on the urban characteristics of the space for consumption, and with reference to opportunities for sociability and retail trade, Michishige describes the historical trajectory of British urban retail-shop trades, focusing on consumption tastes. He analyses those improvements promoted by a rising middle-class in provincial towns to enhance the urban environment: better streets, drainage, sanitation and lighting, along with the growing number of retail shops and changed lay-out of retailing facilities. He also notes two varieties of consumer goods. One was the items of conspicuous consumption, to show off; the other, commodities for daily use in the private sphere. Michishige suggests that social relations structured around retail shops, and shopping as leisure, were developing as salient features of urban culture. This idea is important: the markets were not impersonal, but essentially based on personalized exchange with face-to-face intimate contacts between sellers and customers.

Karasawa deals with the municipal corporation's process of building urban infrastructure in Norwich, East Anglia. Here, a local Improvement Act was obtained later than in many other provincial towns. The Norwich corporation, he argues, showed a deep commitment to the civil life of town dwellers, as a trustee of endowed charities. This effort was in addition to the support of voluntary associations which administered a variety of charities. Thereby, the Norwich corporation contributed to the development of the town's institutional infrastructure. It is also striking that a considerable portion of the town's financial expenditure was invested not only in public sectors such as markets and streets improvements, but also in an urban renaissance represented in cultural activities, including new halls and the 'City Waits' (musical bands).

Emi Konishi's chapter on sociability and 'urban renaissance' considers facilities provided by the municipal corporation, improvement commissioners and commercial entrepreneurs of King's Lynn, one of the largest port-towns in south-east England, and how these altered social exchanges. Town dwellers participated in the public sphere for municipal elections, open marriage ceremonies or funeral services. Konishi suggests that a new kind of sociability emerged during this period, offered by voluntary associations and merchants in the forms of dramas, balls, music concerts, exhibitions, subscription assemblies, entertainments or sports events.

Through an analysis of the court of burgesses, Shūji Sugawara scrutinizes changes in municipal governance in the London district of Westminster during this period of urban renaissance. Merchants and upper-level craftsmen composed the court of burgesses, which had originated in the seigneurial courts. Its jurisdiction ranged from market regulations, housing and streets, to the moral behaviour of inhabitants. Sugawara uses court records to explore whether eighteenth-century Westminster enjoyed a separate urban identity while also being part of a larger city which was strongly influential and speedily expanding outwards. This rapid growth saw the city spill out into the adjoining counties of Middlesex and Surrey, becoming an urban complex of greater London.

Kiyoshi Sakamaki examines a kaleidoscopic multiple power structure in the eighteenth-century Corporation of London, the direct authority of which extended no further than the square mile of the city. His investigation, which analyzes changes in controls exercised by mayors, aldermen and city councillors over legislative, administrative and jurisdictional powers, elaborately reveals a complex municipal system, which was both multi-functional and reciprocal.

The only chapter dealing with a manufacturing town, by Chiaki Yamamoto and Yukihito Morimoto explores the development of self-governance, occupational structures and consumption in Wolverhampton during the urban renaissance. The authors examine the work of improvement commissioners who exerted a great influence on the development of infrastructure. The authors deduce occupational structures, through the investigation of trade directories and criminal records. Their analyses reveal consumption trends as well as a shift from a town focused upon manufacture, to an urban centre with a diversified economy created by the sustained growth of the tertiary sector.

Alongside this bright sides of urbanization, Takeshi Nagashima considers the dark side of urban renaissance set against high mortality, dis-amenities and distress resulting from deteriorating environments caused by mass in-migration and severe congestion. Nagashima's paper on urban penalties and urban renaissance aims to address this seeming incompatibility through a survey of past researches and the latest findings. He suggests that in the eighteenth century, environmental improvements, and a better quality of consumer goods such as clothing, reduced exposure to infectious diseases and thus lowered urban mortality. Nagashima believes these factors to have been more significant than the increased calorie intakes made possible by a tangibly rising standard of living in tandem with higher resistance to disease. He is correct to note that local authorities opposed interference into their autonomy by the central government, for instance in the public health movements led by Edwin Chadwick in the nineteenth century.

Lastly, with a unique viewpoint upon urbanization, independent of conventional approaches which tend to discuss urban history in relation to economic development or industrialization, Yō Kawana traces the path towards urban renaissance in eighteenth-century Britain in a chapter entitled 'Commercialization in the Medieval and Early Modern Urban Process'. Rather than population growth, rise in income or material affluence, Kawana emphasizes the institutional, organizational and cultural aspects of urbanity. In particular, he insists that commercialization, one of the most important *raisons d'être* and functions of urban centres in the Middle Ages and through to the eighteenth century, had a variety of significant effects on the urban setting and landscape.

While adopting a wide range of approaches, most contributors share an academic interest in reconstructing British urban culture in the 'long' eighteenth century, the period intervening between the Middle Ages and the era of rapid industrialization. It was a time when British towns flourished as consumption expanded. The country experienced 'Smithian economic growth', with real wages rising, a variety of demands growing, and markets and the division of labour steadily proceeding. The 'urban renaissance' is an historical symbol of this.

The contents of this book are fresh and challenging, evidence of the current healthy state of Japanese research into British urban history. The work has broad appeal to urban historians researching a range of topics, and the research includes substantial new insights and information. More than this, it suggests the next steps, and some entirely new approaches through which the breadth of the subject can be further explored.

First of all, how did overseas colonies affect the urban renaissance? Their economic benefits would vary town by town, and might deliver different models of domestic 'urban renaissance'. This point has broader significance when considering the shift in urban consumption patterns during the period. While contributors in this volume have tried to pay attention to the rise of consumer society and the spread of consumer culture, as noted in the introduction, few papers refer to the effects of colonization, which need to be better understood in their relation to the British urban renaissance.

Furthermore, urbanization can be seen as providing a space to supply, cluster and consume intellectual commodities, as evinced in the growth of voluntary associations and their sharing of ideas, knowledge or technologies. Such a perspective widens the scope for the historical study of eighteenth-century British urban society.

One editor, Nakano, emphasizes that the difficulties confronting present-day cities globally differ essentially from the experience of British towns during the eighteenth and early-nineteenth centuries. It is revealing that urban problems with which modern cities are struggling in economically and politically matured developed countries are not the same as those accompanying industrialization. It should be noted, though, that some urban centres in developing countries do indeed experience the serious and urgent environmental and other difficulties with which many English towns endeavoured to cope during the 'long' eighteenth century.

Chapter 7
Review of Yoshiyuki Morishita, *Kindai Cheko Jūtaku Shakaishi: Shinkokka no Keisei to Shakaikōsō* (Czech Housing Policy and Social History in the First Half of the Twentieth Century: Building the First Czechoslovak Republic)

Hokkaido University Press, Sapporo, 2013

Nodoka Nagayama

The book analyzes social reform in Czechoslovakia in the first part of the twentieth century by examining the housing policies of political parties and the housing reform movement led by architects.

The book consists of the Introduction, Part I (Chapters 1–3) and Part II (Chapters 4–7).

Part 1, "Experiments with housing estates in the suburbs – from the Imperial Era to the 1920s", addresses social reform from the late Habsburg Empire to the Czechoslovak Republic founded in 1918.

Chapter 1, "Cities, housing and society in Bohemia and Prague under the imperial regime", examines the development of an active housing reform movement. Serious housing problems emerged as the population of Prague and surrounding areas increased in conjunction with industrialization at the end of the nineteenth century. An active housing reform movement emerged in response. The movement was based on the bourgeois ideal of the working class' attaining a middle-class life-style.

Chapter 2, "Housing policy in the first Czechoslovak Republic – seeking to enable the lower classes to follow the middle class path", addresses the legislation in housing policy in the new Czechoslovak Republic. The ruling parties in the new state took countermeasures to prevent the threat of intensifying ethnic conflicts and

---

This is a translation of a book review that originally appeared in *Shakai Keizai Shigaku* 80(3) (November 2014), pp. 144–146.

N. Nagayama (✉)
College of Economics, Aoyama Gakuin University,
4-4-25, Shibuya, Shibuya-ku, 150-8366 Tokyo, Japan
e-mail: nodoka@mbj.ocn.ne.jp

S. Baba (ed.), *Economic History of Cities and Housing*, Monograph Series of the Socio-Economic History Society, Japan, DOI 10.1007/978-981-10-4097-9_7

of proletarian revolution: their social reforms were oriented towards European-style capitalism. The social reform legislation was developed through inter-party cooperation, based on compromise between "the bourgeois parties, which advocated market improvements, and the socialist parties, except for the Communist Party". Housing policy legislation was drafted within the same framework. With these laws, the government gave significant financial support to the housing societies that had been founded under the imperial regime. These societies supported home ownership by independent individuals. In this respect, the new state's housing reform followed the path of the housing reform movement of the Imperial Era, aiming this time for the lower class to follow the middle-class model of "family-based housing".

Chapter 3, "Housing reform in the 1920s – toward a nation focused on individuals", highlights the development of Prague's metropolitan regions in the 1920s. In Prague, "the State Regulation Commission for Prague and Surroundings (SRC)", under the auspices of the government's Ministry of Public Works, engaged in urban planning and housing development in the suburbs. The garden suburbs in Prague "Spořilov" embodied the single family-housing ideal of the Czech "socialistic parties". They aimed at family-based dwelling, not multiple-family dwellings. However, most of residents were middle-class, and it proved difficult to solve Prague's lower-class housing shortage.

Part 2, "From "family-based dwelling" to "smallest dwelling" – housing reform from the 1930s to the postwar period", addresses the search for optimum social policies, from the interwar period to the postwar period. These housing policies differed from the previous bourgeois policies.

Chapter 4, "Housing policies in the period of economic panic – from 'family-based dwelling' to 'smallest dwelling'" discusses the government's criteria for financial aid for housing from the late 1920s to the early 1930s. In this period, the rule parties changed their focus from the 80-m^2 "family-based dwelling" to the 40-m^2, so-called "smallest dwelling". The main opposition party, the Communist Party, consisting of organized workers who did not benefit from any housing policies, requested its own housing policy in Parliament.

Chapter 5, "New housing reform concepts – interwar era activities of the architect's group", highlights the activities of functionalistic architecture. Avant-garde architects and the intelligentsia held themselves apart from the government's housing policy and attempted to refute the conventional ideal of the lower classes attaining a middle-class life-style. Their interest was in communism and Soviet architecture. Most of them were familiar with the Communist Party in Czechoslovakia, but kept their distance from political activity.

Chapter 6, "Housing problems in German districts – community and nation" examines the German housing reform movement, the conflicts among different German parties and the policy that developed under the Nazi regime (1938–1945). The financial aid for minimal dwellings, advocated by Czechoslovakia's government, was denied by the Nazi government because of the increase in the number of these "smallest" dwelling. Instead, the Nazi government supported financial aid for "family-based dwellings." Its settlement policy was also informed by race theory.

Chapter 7, "Housing policies in the Third Republic Era, 1945–1948", deals with postwar housing policies related to the removal of Germans and the settlement of Czech people in the borderland and to the "two-year plan" launched by the postwar government after the settlement. During the "two-year plan" discussions of housing policy, the socialist parties in the government, in tandem with the avant-garde architects, criticized the liberalistic housing market of the prewar era and called for state control of the market. The socialization of housing was also encouraged by those working to achieve equal rights for men and women. Nevertheless, the "family-based dwelling" ideal of the 1920s persisted during this time as well, and the government gradually began to focus on the concept of "family-based dwellings" instead of the socialization of housing.

This book is an ambitious work, analyzing the above areas through an abundant use of archives and publications from Czechoslovakia, and both the Czech and German literature. The author succeeds, particularly in Chapter 3, in describing the result of the housing reform movement from various angles. Taken as a whole, the book merits high regard for two important reasons.

First, the author analyzes the concept of social reform in the context of the foundation of the new state, the first republic founded in 1918. The author focuses on the adoption of parliamentary democracy, which was the new state's most important feature, and carefully analyzes the discussion of social policy in the national and municipal governments, directing his attention to the interests of the different parties. The author's research brings to light both the continuation of imperial-era policies and the cooperation among the parties. Discussions of the foundation of new states often overlook continuities in policy and cooperation, while stressing more negative outcomes such as discontinuity and conflict. Giving due consideration to the documents, the author focuses on the ideal of the lower classes following the middle-class model, and thereby clarifies not only the effect of inter-party cooperation, but also its limitations.

Second, the author places Czechoslovakia's housing reform and architecture not only in its national context, but in relation to the international context as well. Analyzing the acceptance of both Western housing reform and Soviet architecture, he regards Czechoslovakia as a meeting point of Eastern and Western culture and as a mid-point between the two ways of thinking about reform. The book succeeds in using Czechoslovakia's geographic character, lying as it did between Western Europe and the Soviet Union, and illustrating the elements of housing reform and architecture common to both regions. The book provides a large-scale framework for understanding Czechoslovakia's history beyond the framework of Eastern European history.

Two questions arise with regard to the points mentioned above.

First, the process of constructing a cooperative system for addressing housing policy was not analyzed in detail. The book meticulously describes the similar or common points and differences between the parties. It does not clarify, however, the mechanisms that were used to ensure cooperation among them. In the discussion of social policy in general, the author points out that the cooperation was stimulated both by "Peroutka", the extra-Parliamentary mechanism for addressing party interests (p. 59), and by Masaryk's political thought. However, it does not clarify how "Peroutka" and Masaryk's thought were connected to housing reform and the creation of housing policy. Moreover, the discussion of the "Central Society of Housing Reform in Czechoslovakia (Ustredni jednota pro reform buytovou v Ceskoslovenske republic)", which was an association of housing societies, Cabinet ministers and municipal and state representatives, does not explain what influence the organization's network had on the making of housing policy in the national government. Further analysis of the discussions that took place outside of Parliament will enable us to understand which mechanisms supported the parliamentary democracy of the new state.

Second, Czechoslovakia's "originality" relative to Western Europe and the Soviet Union is not concretely explained in this book, although the author regards Czechoslovakia's thinking about housing reform at the time as "original thinking about social reform", meaning "neither liberalism nor socialism" (p. 2, p. 270). Indeed, the author seemingly regards as "originality" the housing in Brno, in which a functional apartment-style housing element was added to the previous idea of "healthy and hygienic family-based dwelling" (p. 189). However, Western countries were already experimenting with such housing in the 1920s. The same is true of the "socialization of housekeeping and child care" (p. 196) advocated by Czechoslovakia's avant-garde architects in the 1930s. Given Western Europe's socialist housing reforms in the early nineteenth century, such as Fourier's experimental housing ("Phalanstère"), Czechoslovakia's attempts do not appear especially original. Czechoslovakia's housing reform should instead be analyzed in the context of the socialist housing reforms developed in Western Europe as well.

Finally, the "development" of Czechoslovakia's society is not thoroughly explained, although it is one of the main themes of this book. A more comprehensive discussion of change and development in Czechoslovakia would provide a stronger framework for understanding Czechoslovakia's history.

Chapter 8
Review of Nodoka Nagayama, *Doitsu Jyūtaku Mondai no Shakai Keizaishi teki Kenkyū*: Fukushi Kokka to Hieiri Jyūtaku Kensetsu (Study on the Socio-economic History of Housing Problems in Germany: Welfare State and Non-profit Housing)

Nihon Keizai Hyōronsha, Tokyo, 2012

Satoshi Baba

The aim of this book is to clarify the characteristics of German housing problems in the 1920s. In the introduction the author shows some fundamental viewpoints. Firstly, she points out that German housing problems in the 1920s should be divided into three components: (1) the deficiency of the housing for low-income classes including manual workers after 1850 (the old type); (2) the deficiency of housing for young couples after World War I (the new type); (3) the housing problem for large families and war victims (the specific type). Secondly, the author takes notice the non-profit (public utility) housing organizations that constructed small housing units and did not aim to make a profit. Thirdly, the author concentrates on researching the case of the city of Solingen where non-profit housing was built most actively among the cities in Germany at that period. Moreover the author stresses some characteristics of the German welfare state, namely: (1) cities were its driving forces; (2) the post-World War I demographic transformation of generations and household composition forced the formation of welfare state; (3) a wide range of social strata was its beneficiary.

Part I "City and Housing" includes four chapters concerning the non-profit housing in Solingen. The history of Solingen since the Middle Ages, especially the

---

This is a translation of a book review that originally appeared in *Shakai Keizai Shigaku* 80(3) (November 2014), pp. 146–148.

S. Baba (✉)
Graduate School of Economics, The University of Tokyo,
7-3-1 Hongo, Bunkyo-ku, 113-0033 Tokyo, Japan
e-mail: sbaba@e.u-tokyo.ac.jp

S. Baba (ed.), *Economic History of Cities and Housing*, Monograph Series of the Socio-Economic History Society, Japan, DOI 10.1007/978-981-10-4097-9_8

development of the metal processing industry was traced in Chapter 1 "Solingen as a city of the metal processing industry". The author makes clear that the grade of mechanization differed according to the processes, and the nearly independent artisans continued to exist especially in the polishing process. The proportion of small enterprises was high. The industrial relations were cooperative, but these relations broke up after 1900.

Chapter 2 "Non-profit housing and the metal processing industry's entrepreneurs" discusses the financial support of local entrepreneurs to the non-profit housing. The enterprises in Solingen were medium and small in terms of size and specialized in the metal processing industry. For that reason the entrepreneurs were interested in local welfare and supported non-profit housing organizations financially. Though the "Solingen saving housing society (SBV)", a main research object of this book, was established in 1889, its achievement was not significant before World War I. From the 1920s the number of members and the amount of capital increased and a part of the rent tax revenue and the support from the municipality were used increasingly to construct the non-profit housing.

Chapter 3 "Non-profit housing and the city council" clarifies why non-profit housing was actively addressed in Solingen by analyzing the documents of the city council. The majority of Solingen's city councilors were composed from the civil parties like the People's Party or the Democratic Party, not the left-wing parties like the Social Democratic Party (SPD) or the communist party. The civil parties, however, accepted the activity of SBV because the housing problem was serious. The main financial resource was rent tax, and the non-profit organization received 75% of this resource, because Hermann Meyer, the SBV's director-general and an SPD councilor, had great influence on the city council.

Chapter 4 discusses "the activity of the non-profit builder Bauhütte" that was an important actor of the non-profit housing. It was established based on the free trade union under the influence of SPD, and constructed small housing units, following the terms of the social housing enterprise league (VsB). The private builder organization, however, criticized that Bauhütte constructed also other types of housing. Therefore, the VsB omitted the clause of public utility from its terms. Nevertheless "public utility" was emphasized in Solingen even after the revision of the terms, because the city promoted the project with strong cooperation with the SBV.

Part II of the book, "Non-profit housing and the low-income classes (artisans and manual workers)" sheds light on "the new type of housing problem". In Chapter 1 "Non-profit housing and the rented house market", the author emphasizes that not only the old type of housing problem but also the new one should be examined for investigation of the housing problem in the 1920s, and the significance of the non-profit housing should be evaluated in this regard. In the early 1920s the city made an effort to secure the used houses for rent. But the construction of new houses was needed in order to activate the used house market. In Solingen the activity of SBV increased in the late 1920s owing to the financial aid from the city. The construction of the Wegerhof settlement was a reaction to the increase of households which was caused by marriage and separation from parents. This settlement could not resolve the old type of housing problem directly, but as a result of moving to it, the new lodgers came to the empty houses for rent (the infiltration effect), and the old type of housing problem was eventually resolved.

The major residents in the Wegerhof settlement were people from the middle class. But some working class people could live there as minority residents, and became also the beneficiaries of the welfare state. The author searches for reasons for the inclusion of working-class people in the Wegerhof settlement residents in Chapter 2 "Non-profit housing and manual workers". She deduces that the main reason was the reduction of income disparity at the same time, however, it is not negligible that Meyer acceded to the civil housing reform movement which aimed to provide a "moral" living environment to artisans and manual workers. But the author takes particular notice of the fact that the increase of the total income of household members in the Wegerhof settlement made it possible to move into newly-built houses.

Part III of the book, "Municipal housing policy and the socially vulnerable in Solingen" discusses a specific type of housing problem in Solingen. Chapter 1 "Housing supply to war victims and large families" examines how the German welfare state carried out the policy which had become a pressing issue as a result of World War I. Such people were treated preferentially in the delivery of various subsidies, and the Reich, states and municipalities responded to the demands of related associations preferentially. In Solingen too, the city, together with the SBV, provided the housing to war victims and large families earnestly, and this specific type of housing problem was mitigated.

Chapter 2 "Accommodations for homeless people and a minimum standard of living" examines the city's direct mediation of accommodations for homeless people. A facility for the homeless in Solingen was called Gosolei. It accepted both actual and potential homeless people. Therefore it functioned as a facility for preventing the increase of homelessness at the same time. Though conditions at the Gosolei were poor, the rent was cheap, and some people were able to move from the Gosolei to municipal housing if they were able to receive mediation from the city. In this sense it can be said that non-profit housing for various classes of people had codependent and complementary relationships with the city's housing policy for the socially vulnerable.

In a special section of the book, "Supplement: small housing development in the early Nazi period", the author discusses German housing policy at that period taking the case of Cologne for example. She explains the differences of this policy from that of the Weimar period.

In the Conclusion of the book, the author summarizes the contents of this book and stresses that her analysis establishes the hypothesis that cities' activities and their reactions to the changes in the composition of generations and households led to the welfare state type of housing policy.

The first merit of this book is that by using primary sources and focusing on the example of Solingen, the author clarifies in detail the various aspects of the non-profit housing which characterize German housing policy in the 1920s. Especially the occupation, stratum and family composition is analyzed carefully.

Secondly, it is noteworthy that the author divides housing problems into three types: the old type, the new type and the specific type, and inquires into the relation between these types. As a result she succeeds in understanding the German housing problem in the 1920s more deeply than previous studies have done.

Thirdly, the author stresses the reason for the emergence of the German welfare state in the 1920s in the state housing policy as a result of the transformation of generation and household composition, and makes note of the beneficiaries of welfare state policy.

The reviewer, however, has doubt that the detailed analysis on housing policy in Solingen necessarily leads to the overgeneralized conclusions about the importance of non-profit housing in German housing construction and about the emergence of the German welfare state.

Firstly, it is easy to understand that Solingen is a typical example of German housing policy, because the proportion of non-profit housing in the new-built housing in the 1920s was high. Solingen, however, was a typical middle-sized city that had an industrial structure based on the metal processing industry, the predominance of middle-sized enterprises and the strong ties of the Social Democratic Party with SBV. Therefore, it is necessary to compare these factors with those of other German cities in order to generalize conclusions drawn from the example of Solingen.

Secondly, the term "city as a driving force" of a welfare state is misleading. The non-profit housing in Solingen was executed in the special environment of the cooperation of SBV and public organizations like the council, in addition to Bauhütte and private enterprises. The author also utilizes the expression "policies and activities of the city". The city should be regarded not as a "driving force", but as a stage where the activities of various actors were performed.

Thirdly, a hypothesis that "the transformation of generation and household composition" produced new type of housing problem, and the reaction to the problem led to the housing policy of welfare state is stimulating. The reviewer agrees that the policymakers acknowledged the increase of marriages and household numbers in the 1920s. The housing policy of the welfare state, however, started from the 1950s, and was in full swing in this decade. It is not deniable that the fact that the provision of housing funds from the central government based on the rent tax contributed to the realization of the non-profit housing in the 1920s. The author stresses a trend toward nuclear families. But families of manual workers could live in the Wegerhof settlement since they were organized as the old type of family; that is, children living together with parents also added to the household income. Indeed it is an interesting fact, but it seems that the author overemphasizes "the transformation of generation and household composition" as a factor in the establishment of the welfare-state housing policy.

Fourthly, what is "(possible) wide range of social strata" as beneficiary of the housing policy? It is a problem for the author too. But it remains unclear exactly who the beneficiary were: young couples, low-income strata including manual workers, middle classes or other strata. The task of the social state is that the state assumes people's "existence precaution (Daseinsvorsorge)" including that of upper social strata which don't need "social assistance". But the social (welfare) state researches tend to concentrate on the people which need it. In the opinion of the reviewer, it is a cause of confusion.

This book has the above-mentioned problems. Nevertheless, it is an excellent book in terms of proofs and viewpoints, and it is a great contribution to the research fields of German housing history, urban history and the history of the German welfare state.

Index

S. Baba (ed.), *Economic History of Cities and Housing*, Monograph Series of the Socio-Economic History Society, Japan, DOI 10.1007/978-981-10-4097-9

FSC
www.fsc.org
MIX
Papier | Fördert gute Waldnutzung
FSC® C083411

Kolibri 360 GmbH
Ferdinand-Jühlke-Straße 7
99095 Erfurt, Deutschland
produktsicherheit@kolibri360.de